Socrates Meets Kant

Other Works of Peter Kreeft from St. Augustine's Press

Philosophy 101 by Socrates
Socrates Meets Descartes
Socrates Meets Freud
Socrates Meets Hume
Socrates Meets Kierkegaard
Socrates Meets Machiavelli
Socrates Meets Marx
Socrates Meets Sartre
The Philosophy of Jesus
Jesus-Shock
Summa Philosophica
Socratic Logic
Socrates' Children: Ancient
Socrates' Children: Medieval
Socrates' Children: Modern
Socrates' Children: Contemporary
Socrates' Children [all four books in one]
An Ocean Full of Angels
The Sea Within
I Surf, Therefore I Am
If Einstein Had Been a Surfer

Socrates Meets Kant

The Father of Philosophy Meets His Most Influential Modern Child

A Socratic Cross-Examination of Kant's *Critique of Pure Reason* and *Foundations of the Metaphysics of Morals*

By Peter Kreeft

ST. AUGUSTINE'S PRESS
South Bend, Indiana

Manufactured in the United States of America

1 2 3 4 5 6   20 19 18 17 16 15 14

Library of Congress Control Number: 2020935700

✕ The paper used in this publication meets the minimum requirements of
the American National Standard for Information Sciences Permanence of
Paper for Printed Materials, ANSI Z39.481984

ST. AUGUSTINE'S PRESS
www.staugustine.net

For Ronald K. Tacelli

Contents

Preface

This book is one in a series of Socratic explorations of some of the Great Books. Books in this series are intended to be short, clear, and nontechnical, thus fully understandable by beginners. They also introduce (or review) the basic questions in the fundamental divisions of philosophy (see the chapter titles): metaphysics, epistemology, anthropology, ethics, logic, and method. They are designed both for classroom use and for educational do-it-yourselfers. The "Socrates Meets . . ." books can be read and understood completely on their own, but each is best appreciated after reading the little classic it engages in dialogue.

The setting—Socrates and the author of the Great Book meeting in the afterlife—need not deter readers who do not believe there is an afterlife. For although the two characters and their philosophies are historically real, their conversation, of course, is not and requires a "willing suspension of disbelief". There is no reason the skeptic cannot extend this literary belief also to the setting.

Introduction

Kant is really two philosophers: (1) the epistemologist of *The Critique of Pure Reason* and (2) the ethicist of the *Grounding for for the Metaphysics of Morals* [sometimes translated as *The Foundations of the Metaphysics of Morals* or *Fundamental Principles of the Metaphysic of Morals*]. That's why this book is almost twice as long as the others in the *Socrates Meets* series. That's also why I have modified Socrates' style of argument a little bit and made it more short and direct than it is in Plato.

It is also longer because Kant is probably the most important philosopher since Thomas Aquinas. If he had written only half of what he wrote—*either* half, the epistemology or the ethics—he would still be the most important and influential of all modern philosophers. As it is, his epistemology is truly the "Copernican revolution in philosophy", as he termed it: the most fundamental revolution in the whole history of epistemology; and his ethics is the most important one since Aristotle's. No other modern philosopher can rival his influence in either field, much less both. Only the revolution of Descartes in epistemology and the revolution of Nietzsche in ethics might be thought to rival that of Kant in being radical. Yet Descartes' epistemological revolution was radical mainly in method rather than content, and it only paved the way for Kant's much more radical, "Copernican" one; and Kant's revolution in ethics was the necessary foundation to (unwittingly) pave the way for Nietzsche's extreme reaction against it.

There are thinkers who accept the essential claims of Kant's epistemology but not his ethics. There are thinkers who accept his ethics but not his epistemology. There are thinkers who accept both. And there are thinkers who reject the fundamental claims of both. This book is critical of Kant in both areas (though not equally critical: it is more critical of the epistemology than of the ethics) because that is what I think the position of the historical Socrates would be. Yet at the same time I think he would recognize Kant's greatness, genius, genuine contributions, and profound rightness on many points.

My exploration of Kant's ethics, in the second half of this book, is a close reading of the key passages in the *Grounding for the Metaphysics of Morals* in a kind of Oxford-tutorial type of Socratic cross-examination, as in my other "Socrates Meets . . ." books; and this is writable and readable because the *Grounding for the Metaphysics of Morals* is a conveniently short and readable book. But my exploration of Kant's epistemology, in the first half of this book, is *not* a close reading of *The Critique of Pure Reason*, for that book is far too difficult for the beginning student to tackle, and far too long. It is also written in a heavy Germanic academic style that contrasts unfavorably both with the classical lucidity of other Enlightenment writers like Descartes, Hume, Voltaire, or Mill, and with the emotional enthusiasm and poetic eloquence of nearly all anti-Enlightenment writers, whether Conservatives like Burke or Romanticists like Rousseau or Existentialists like Kierkegaard and Nietzsche. So in the first, epistemological, half of this book I have merely summarized the most influential and revolutionary conclusions and arguments in *The Critique of Pure Reason*. This whole book, but especially the first half of it, is designed not for a dialogue with scholars but for the education of intelligent beginners in philosophy.

Many philosophers write long, difficult books and also shorter, more popular summaries of them. For instance, Sartre wrote not only *Being and Nothingness* but also *Existentialism and Human Emotions*. Hume wrote not only the *Essay* but also the *Enquiry*. Descartes wrote not only the *Meditations* but also the *Discourse on Method*. Marx wrote not only *Capital* but also *The Communist Manifesto*. Machiavelli wrote not only the *Discourses* but also *The Prince*. (And all five of these shorter, easier books are the subject of "Socrates Meets . . ." books in this series.) Kant too wrote not only the long and difficult *Critique of Practical Reason* but also the short and relatively easy *Grounding for the Metaphysics of Morals*. But Kant never wrote a clear and easy book in epistemology, though he did write a fairly short one, namely, the *Prolegomena to Any Future Metaphysics*. But both the literary style and the logical arguments in that book make it as difficult to read as the original, much longer *Critique of Pure Reason*. Beginners will despair; I do not want beginners to despair.

The Critique of Pure Reason is the most important philosophical book of modern times. It must be understood, and evaluated, even though it is one of the most difficult of all books to understand and therefore to evaluate. I found only one solution to this dilemma: to summarize the *Critique*, without expecting students to read it, before exploring the much more readable *Grounding for the Metaphysics of Morals*.

I

Introducing Kant Himself

KANT: (awakening after death, assessing his situation, and musing aloud). It seems I was both right and wrong about the afterlife. The soul is indeed immortal, as I believed. But apparently the body is too. And . . . it seems I am not alone. Who is this who comes to greet me? An angel? He is robed in white. But he is short and fat and ugly. He looks less like an angel than like a flatfish. Could it possibly be . . . Socrates?

SOCRATES: It could indeed quite possibly be that I am I. Unless the law of noncontradiction has been abolished—which is impossible, as you yourself well understood.

KANT: Is that supposed to be a joke or serious?

SOCRATES: Couldn't it be both?

KANT: You do sound like Socrates indeed. What is this strange place? And what are we doing here? I notice you are speaking Greek and I am speaking German, and yet the speech of both of us comes out in English. How does that happen? And why do we instantly understand each other?

SOCRATES: Because we are now in a place, or a time, where the Tower of Babel has been undone by the events of Pentecost.

KANT: Am I then in Heaven with the saints?

SOCRATES: Not quite. You may call it Purgatory.

KANT: I did not believe in that Catholic doctrine. The term does not sit well with me.

SOCRATES: Call it what you will, you will still have to endure its trials, beginning with my own cross-examination of your thoughts.

KANT: If this is true, and if that is the only trial I have to endure, then this is a happy trial indeed to me. Philosophical conversation with Socrates does not seem to merit the label of "Purgatory" at all.

SOCRATES: Perhaps after a while, and after a few passes between us, you will change your mind about that.

KANT: No, I think not. For like you, Socrates, I philosophized only for truth, not for victory. If your cross-examination proves my philosophy to be false, I will not complain but only thank you for the great gift of leading me to the truth. And if it proves my philosophy to be true, I will do exactly the same thing.

SOCRATES: I know you speak truly, my noble friend, for in this place it is impossible for either of us to lie.

KANT: Then let us begin our happy task. Ask away, O master of the philosophical question. And I shall try to defend myself.

SOCRATES: But I will not necessarily be attacking you, only examining you. Or rather, your ideas. A question is not necessarily a weapon of destruction, you know.

KANT: But in your hands it usually was, Socrates.

SOCRATES: Not always. If you recall my conversation with the great Parmenides, you will remember that in that dialogue I learned far more than I taught and lost more arguments than I won. And you may well be as formidable as Parmenides.

KANT: But that conversation was fictional, was it not?

SOCRATES: Why do you think so?

KANT: Because if the historians are right, the real Parmenides died before you were old enough to hold a philosophical conversation with him.

SOCRATES: That is true. Yet a man's philosophy may outlive the man, and therefore we can hold a conversation with a philosophy even after the philosopher is dead. In fact, that is what all readers of this book are doing right now.

KANT: Are you telling me that we are only fictional characters in a book?

SOCRATES: I did not say "only" and I did not say "fictional".

KANT: Can you then explain . . . ?

SOCRATES: I can, but I will not. For we have more important questions to explore.

KANT: Since you have apparently been appointed by higher powers to be the host, and the master of the conversation, I will accept your will in this matter.

SOCRATES: How polite and compliant a gentleman you are! And that may be a good way for us to begin:

to ask what made such a compliant man as you such a philosophical revolutionary. If you don't mind, I will begin by reading to you from your fellow citizen Heinrich Heine, the poet who summarized your importance to the world in these puzzling words:

H 136

> The history of the life of Immanuel Kant is hard to write, inasmuch as he had neither life nor history, for he lived a mechanically ordered, abstract old bachelor life in a quiet retired street in Königsberg, an old town on the northeast border of Germany. I do not believe that the great clock in the cathedral there did its daily work more impassionately and regularly than its compatriot Immanuel Kant. Rising, coffee-drinking, writing, reading college lectures, eating, walking, had all their fixed time, and the neighbors knew that it was exactly half-past three when Immanuel Kant in his grey coat, with his Manilla cane in his hand, left his house door and went to the lime tree Avenue, which is still called in memory of him the Philosopher's Walk. . . .

KANT: What a nice tribute! This is all true, and accurate, and . . .

SOCRATES: But wait! Hear what Heine says next:

H V, 136–37

> Strange contrast between the external life of the man and his destroying, world-crushing thoughts! In very truth, if the citizens of Königsberg had dreamed of the real meaning of his thought, they would have experienced at his sight a greater horror than they would on beholding an executioner, who only kills men. But the good people saw nothing in him but a professor of philo-

sophy, and when he at his regular hour passed   H 137
by, they greeted him as a friend, and regulated
their watches by him.

But . . . Immanuel Kant, the great destroyer
in the world of thought, went far beyond Maxi-
milian Robespierre in terrorism . . . one placed
a king, and the other a god in the scales. . . .

And they both gave exact weight.

KANT: But that is absurd! I was no atheist or any kind
of destroyer. Why does he use that word?

SOCRATES: I think he is referring to your destruction
of reason.

KANT: But as I explained, I destroyed not reason but
only its false pretensions, and I did so only to make
room for faith. I also dispute the poet's version of
my personality. He makes me look like a mechanical
clock, not a man of flesh and blood.

SOCRATES: Well, you did live a clockwork life, did
you not, in both space and time? You hardly ever
left your native Königsberg. Your schedule was exact: waking at exactly five A.M. every morning, working at your desk until seven, lecturing or tutoring in
the morning, returning to your study until one P.M.,
taking your one meal of the day then, followed by a
walk, no matter what the weather was.

KANT: You apparently know all the details of my life.
You know, then, also that I often had hearty and very
human conversations at mealtime.

SOCRATES: Yes indeed. I also know that you always
walked alone because you believed that conversation
should never take place in the open air because it

causes a man to breathe through the mouth instead of the nose.

KANT: But that is true . . . isn't it?

SOCRATES: You also hated noise, moving your bachelor's lodging twice to avoid neighbors, and once writing a letter to the police complaining about the loud hymns sung by the inmates of a nearby prison.

KANT: Hating noise is fairly common among men, Socrates.

SOCRATES: You also hated music, except for military marches. Do you know what Shakespeare said about people who had no music in their souls?

KANT: Is this an inquisition?

SOCRATES: Do you not see the twinkle in my eye?

KANT: You are having a little laugh at my expense.

SOCRATES: Exactly. You may have as many laughs at my expense as you wish. For I was even uglier, shorter, and more eccentric than you, in my own way. Except that I had a wife and children.

KANT: I contemplated marriage twice.

SOCRATES: And both times you hesitated long enough to ensure your state of bachelorhood.

KANT: But I wrote admiring things about women when I was young, almost twenty years before publishing my first book, *The Critique of Pure Reason*, in 1781, at the age of fifty-seven.

P Corr   SOCRATES: Indeed. But not about marriage, which
235   you described as **"an agreement between two peo-**

ple for the reciprocal use of each other's sexual organs".

KANT: That was in a letter, not a book.

SOCRATES: But it was from your mind, was it not?

KANT: Yes.

SOCRATES: And does one man have one mind, as he has one head, or two minds, as he has two hands?

KANT: One.

SOCRATES: Can we then expect to find some connections, at least, between that man's ideas about human knowledge and human morality and that man's ideas about marriage, or schedules, or music?

KANT: Yes, especially since, as I supposed, it is necessary to posit a transcendental unity of apperception, a single enduring subject behind all experience, and which Hume denied, but which I showed could be believed even though it is not a possible object of experience. . . .

SOCRATES: Oh, dear. If you go on like that, I fear you will lose me. I have far too simple a mind to think such abstract thoughts without concrete examples, and to comprehend such technical terminology without clear definitions, and to combine so many diverse questions in a single thought without logically cross-examining each, one at a time. And since I am quite incapable of understanding your style of writing and speaking, while I am sure that you, like anyone else, can easily understand mine, I must insist that we use my method and style rather than yours.

KANT: It seems I must accept these rules. For you seem to be the master of this place, whatever it is. At least, you are the host and I am your guest. So I will try to live by the rules of your house.

SOCRATES: Thank you, Immanuel. You are a gracious and kindly man.

KANT: Thank you for saying so, Socrates. I feared you were here as my judge rather than as my friend.

SOCRATES: I am indeed your friend. Your Judge you will meet much later, on a far higher level than this. But I am also a judge in a sense—not of you but of your ideas. And that is precisely my way of being your friend.

KANT: I understand. And I am ready to proceed.

2

Kant's Place in
the History of Philosophy

SOCRATES: Let's begin not with arguments or texts but with a little of the historical background that we need to understand them. Where did you see yourself fitting into the history of Western philosophy? What were the pressing philosophical questions of your day? To what point had "the great conversation" progressed when you entered it?

KANT: I will be glad to summarize this, Socrates. I am glad you want to understand me, and not just criticize me, and I am glad you understand that this must be done historically as well as logically. To understand my answers you must understand my questions, for nothing is more meaningless than an answer to a question that you do not ask, or do not understand, or do not care about.

SOCRATES: Please proceed, then, and please do not mind if I interrupt you with questions. This is not a lecture but a dialogue, after all. But for now, I want mainly to listen, not to argue.

KANT: Good. Well, I had been educated in the philosophy of Christian von Wolff, who was a disciple of

Leibniz. Wolff was an intelligent and respectable Rationalist philosopher, though rather unoriginal and uninspired. Leibniz, in turn, was one of the greatest geniuses in the history of human thought, perhaps the last universal genius. He was also a Rationalist, as was Descartes, Leibniz' primary influence and model in philosophy. Descartes was another great genius who is deservedly called "the father of modern philosophy".

SOCRATES: Perhaps we should first define "Rationalism".

KANT: Indeed. I was getting to that. I think we should distinguish two senses of the word. In the broad sense, I never ceased to be a Rationalist. But in the narrow sense, I was converted away from Rationalism by the arguments of David Hume.

Let us take the broad sense first. Like most philosophers in my day, I was very much a part of the movement called the "Enlightenment", which saw science and the scientific method as a bright new hope for mankind to settle its old disputes and to progress into eras of not only scientific and technological progress but also human, humane, moral progress. We were animated by the hope that if we applied the more rigorously rational methods and the more open and unprejudiced attitudes of science to the problems of philosophy and morality and politics and even religion, we could overcome ancient superstitions, prejudices, and wars and significantly increase human happiness on this earth, perhaps even for ever, with no limit to this progress. This is the broad sense of "Rationalism".

The narrow sense is a particular answer to the primary question of epistemology, How do we find truth? Or, more specifically, how do we find certainty? And Rationalism's answer is: by pure reason, not by sense experience.

SOCRATES: You realize, of course, that that question contains an assumption.

KANT: It assumes that we *can* attain certainty.

SOCRATES: Yes. Should we not therefore reformulate the question? For there were skeptics around in your day, as there were in mine, who would *not* make that assumption.

KANT: Yes indeed. So then let us reformulate the question—the fundamental question of epistemology—as: "How best can I know?" or "How can I approach most closely to certainty about the truth?"

SOCRATES: You are asking *two* questions here, are you not? About knowing truth and about knowing it with certainty.

KANT: Yes, and we should distinguish those two questions. For certainty presupposes truth—we cannot attain certainty about anything else except truth—but truth does not presuppose certainty, for we can know the truth without knowing it with certainty. Indeed, there seem to be many things of which we have only probable knowledge—what you called "right opinion", Socrates—while there seem to be other things of which we have certain knowledge.

SOCRATES: So we should not *assume* that the skeptic is wrong at the outset.

KANT: No. Perhaps the skeptic is right and we really have no certain knowledge at all. But we at least *seem* to have it. And the *concept* of it, the *ideal* of it, is clear in our minds, at least.

SOCRATES: I fear I must demur. I, at least, am not clear and certain that the concept of certainty is clear. Perhaps we should make some very basic distinctions about knowing in order to distinguish the question of certainty from a number of other questions. In fact, I see no less than *four* other questions that might be confused with the question of certainty. I see these other questions surrounding the question of certainty, so to speak, as if the five questions were marching in a certain order. Two of these questions precede the question of certainty and two follow it.

KANT: What questions do you have in mind?

SOCRATES: I think we must distinguish at least five different questions about anything—anything at all.

First, does it exist? Is it real?

Second, if it does exist, do we know it? For surely, unless we are all-knowing, like God, there are some things that are real but unknown to us.

Third, if we know it, is our knowledge certain rather than merely probable?

Fourth, if the knowledge is certain to me, can I make it certain to you by a compelling proof or demonstration? Perhaps there are some certainties that are private and not demonstrable.

Fifth, if there is such a proof or demonstration, is it a scientific proof? Does it use the new, modern scientific method that has made the enterprise of modern science so spectacularly successful? Or is

the proof prescientific, or premodern, or philosophical rather than scientific—like the proofs I offered
in my dialogues? For surely not *all* the proofs offered as demonstrative by all the philosophers in the
world before the scientific method was discovered
were worthless.

KANT: Your ranking of these five questions seems
quite commonsensical, Socrates. Yet I would not order them in this way. In putting the question of being first and the question of knowing second, you are
putting metaphysics first and epistemology second. I
would begin with epistemology, reversing that order.

SOCRATES: I expected you would say that. For that
would seem to be a basic difference between nearly
all premodern philosophies and nearly all modern
philosophies. The ancients all do metaphysics first
and the moderns all, or nearly all, do epistemology
first.

Do you mean that you would put epistemology first
simply as a *method*, as Descartes did when he said we
should check our mental tools first before constructing our mental buildings? Or do you mean something
more than that?

KANT: Both for method and for something more, I
think. First of all, I do agree with Descartes in pre-
ferring the modern method of beginning with epistemology rather than the ancient method of beginning
with metaphysics.

SOCRATES: Why?

KANT: Because I want to be critical rather than naïve.
To do epistemology first is to begin not by *assuming*
the validity of knowledge, but demanding to *prove* it.

Surely you would agree with me there, Socrates; you loved to question all assumptions.

SOCRATES: Indeed I did. But one of the assumptions I would question is the assumption that we can and should begin by questioning all assumptions.

KANT: What do you mean by that?

SOCRATES: I mean simply that Descartes' "methodic doubt" is not the *only* way to begin philosophy. We could also begin it with a kind of "methodic faith", so to speak.

KANT: What would that mean?

SOCRATES: It would mean provisionally accepting the opinions of the other person, or of the consensus, or of common sense, and then questioning that faith, as I did with my dialogue partners.

But we are not here to discuss my method but yours. Tell me, then, about your reason for ranking epistemology before metaphysics. Was your reason for doing this merely to be more critical and to question more assumptions?

KANT: No. There was more than merely a method involved in my asking about knowledge first rather than about being, and doing epistemology prior to metaphysics. In fact, it involved the central and most revolutionary idea of my philosophy, the one Heinrich Heine was probably thinking of when he called me the "destroyer".

SOCRATES: And what idea is that?

KANT: That we have no access to being as it is in itself, as it really is, but only to being as it is able to be known by the reason. And this reason is limited and has a definite structure. So whatever is not fitted into that structure is not knowable by that reason. I tried to map that structure in my first and most important work, *The Critique of Pure Reason*, and thus limit the borders of possible human knowledge more severely than had been done before.

SOCRATES: It seems, then, that you limited human knowledge even more than Hume did, and that you were therefore even more of a skeptic than he was. He believed that the senses, at least, gave us access to the sensible reality as it really is. But you said that we cannot know *any* reality as it really is in itself.

KANT: No, I am not more skeptical than Hume. I *answered* Hume's skepticism with my epistemology.

SOCRATES: How could this be if you limited the range of knowledge more than he did?

KANT: By my most revolutionary idea, which I called my "Copernican revolution in philosophy". The idea is essentially this: that being—the being we know— conforms to our knowledge rather than our knowledge conforming to being; that in knowing, the known object conforms to the knowing subject rather than vice versa; that all the form, or intelligible content, of our knowledge comes from us rather than from the world.

But this is as it should be, and as it must be; so even though we do not know "things in themselves", our knowledge performs its job quite adequately, so there is no reason to be a skeptic. It is wrong to label my philosophy skeptical, or to say I am more of a skeptic than Hume.

SOCRATES: We must soon investigate this most important of all your ideas, your "Copernican revolution in philosophy", much more carefully, Immanuel. But for now I think we should return to your intellectual history, so that we can understand *why* you arrived at this revolutionary idea.

KANT: This is indeed how we should proceed, for this idea was my solution to a problem, and that problem emerged from my historical situation. On the one hand, like everyone else, I was influcnced by the Rationalism of Descartes, in my case filtered through Leibniz and Wolff. On the other hand, I was influenced by the critical Empiricism of Hume, which he inherited from Bacon, Hobbes, Locke, and Berkeley, but which he carried much further than they did into skepticism.

SOCRATES: Empiricism means essentially the reduction of all knowledge to sensation, does it not?

KANT: Yes. Or the reliance on sensation alone, or the testing of all claims to knowledge by sensation, or the priority of sensation.

SOCRATES: So Rationalism and Empiricism were the two answers to the question of epistemology that were in direct combat with each other in your time?

KANT: Yes, and I could accept neither one of them. This is why I had to develop a radically new answer to the question of epistemology, a third way.

SOCRATES: And the question of epistemology that you claimed to answer was—what, exactly?

KANT: It was essentially two questions: "How does our knowledge work?" and "How can we attain real certainty?"

SOCRATES: And why did you reject both Rationalism and Empiricism as answers to those two questions?

KANT: I had opposite reasons for rejecting those two opposite extremes. I called Rationalism "dogmatic philosophy" and Empiricism "skeptical philosophy". I came to see that Rationalism always dogmatically presupposed something that could not be proved— something like "innate ideas"—thus violating its own supposedly scientific, critical method, which claimed to begin with universal methodic doubt, as Descartes said. And Empiricism, as it culminated in Hume, always and necessarily led to skepticism, and that involved a skepticism even of the fundamental principles of physical science, such as the principle of causality. So both philosophies seemed to me to be, in opposite ways, contrary to science.

SOCRATES: Hmmm. From a large, historical perspective, it seems to me that your age was very much like the Middle Ages in some ways. . . .

KANT: What? How can you say that? If there was any age we wanted to distinguish ourselves from, it was the Middle Ages!

SOCRATES: As scientists, of course. But as philosophers too?

KANT: Yes, as philosophers too.

SOCRATES: Why?

KANT: Because medieval thinkers were uncritical. They all accepted Christian theology as divine revelation and used this as a norm for philosophy. And the same was true for Jewish and Muslim philosophy: if anything in philosophy contradicted theology, it was rejected without question. They also accepted theology as the standard for philosophy. The more friendly to theology their philosophy was, the better.

SOCRATES: But that is exactly why it seems to me that your "age of Enlightenment" was very much like the Middle Ages. All you have to do is substitute "Newtonian science" for "Christian theology" and you have the starting point of every single philosopher of the "Enlightenment", both Rationalists and Empiricists. Science was for you both the external and the internal norm of philosophy. If a philosophy contradicted Newtonian science, or even imperiled it, that fact alone was sufficient to refute it. And Newtonian science was the standard for all your philosophical systems. Hume even said, at the beginning of his *Enquiry*, that he hoped to do for human knowing what Newton had done for the external universe.

KANT: This is a very strange way of looking at the Enlightenment. It is not how we saw ourselves at all.

SOCRATES: I realize that. Is it not possible that you did not see yourselves truly? Is it not possible that you were more uncritical than you thought? Is it not possible that I was more skeptical than you were about how easy it is to "know thyself"?

KANT: But the Enlightenment expanded everything. It gave us more knowledge, more options, and more freedom . . .

SOCRATES: Toward the future?

KANT: Yes.

SOCRATES: What about toward the past?

KANT: What do you mean by that?

SOCRATES: Did you have the freedom to embrace the known past as well as the unknown future? Could you look backward as well as forward for "enlightenment"?

KANT: I still do not know exactly what you mean by that.

SOCRATES: Perhaps we can see it if we ask a few more questions. Your immediate problem in epistemology was that Rationalism was too dogmatic and Empiricism was too skeptical, isn't that right?

KANT: Yes.

SOCRATES: Were there no other epistemologies as alternatives?

KANT: Not that I knew of. Either you begin with abstract reason or with concrete sensation. Either you trust reason as your way to certainty, and mistrust the senses until they are validated by reason, as Descartes did; or else you begin by trusting and using the senses and mistrust reason when it is not wholly dependent on sensation and verified by sensation, as Empiricism did. That certainly seems like an either/or.

SOCRATES: Why could there not have been some way to combine these two powers, reason and sensation, instead of simply prioritizing one over the other?

KANT: That is exactly what I tried to find in my new epistemology: a way to combine them.

SOCRATES: Were you aware that this had been done before?

KANT: My epistemology done before? When? By whom?

SOCRATES: No, not your epistemology, not your new *way* of uniting reason and the senses, but your *goal* of uniting reason and the senses.

KANT: I know of no modern philosopher who did that.

SOCRATES: I did not say "modern philosopher", just "philosopher".

KANT: Oh. Old Aristotle, you mean? And Thomas Aquinas?

SOCRATES: Yes. Were you not free to look at that option? Or even Plato? Perhaps he was not simply a primitive version of Descartes.

KANT: But they were premodern.

SOCRATES: Do you tell the truth with a calendar?

KANT: Of course not. But premodern philosophers were uncritical.

SOCRATES: What, exactly, do you mean by that?

KANT: They did not raise the new critical question, as Descartes did, the question of the justification of human reason. Once that question is raised, it must be answered. It cannot be ignored.

SOCRATES: So you thought Plato and Aristotle and Aquinas were even more uncritical than Descartes and the Rationalists because they did metaphysics without doing epistemology first?

KANT: Yes. They simply *assumed* that the human mind could know being, could know reality as it really is, could know "things-in-themselves", as I called them. But in modern philosophy we are more critical: we demand that that assumption be proved, not assumed, or at least that it be justified by being clearly explained —it must be explained *how* we can attain this high goal of a certain knowledge of objective reality.

SOCRATES: I see. But what if it turned out that this question could not be answered ever, at all, in any way, either in the Rationalists' way, or in the Empiricists' way, or in your way, or in any other way?

KANT: What a fantastic hypothesis! Why might that be so?

SOCRATES: Perhaps the question itself presupposes something that is questionable—that reason can get outside itself and validate itself, that it can be both judge and accused prisoner, as it were. Suppose we discover that the assumption this "critical question" presupposes is *self-contradictory?* What would that do to the philosophies that begin with that question?

KANT: Oh. Then of course all philosophies that began with this question would be under suspicion. But do you claim that this is so? Do you say that a self-contradiction is presupposed by this question?

It seems to be a very honest, natural, obvious question, one that our minds of themselves are naturally impelled to ask once we reach a certain age, whether as individuals or as the whole human race: *How do we know* that our reason knows the truth? How do we justify our knowing? Do you see anything wrong with my very question, the critique of reason, even before you investigate my answer to it?

SOCRATES: I do not see anything before I look. But I think we should look, just in case it *is* there, rather than assuming that it *cannot* be there. Do you not agree? Would not that be the more "critical" thing to do?

KANT: I am suspicious of your suspicion, Socrates. Are you trying to put my whole philosophy under a cloud of suspicion before you begin to investigate it? And is this because you have an alternative answer of your own to these questions—perhaps Plato's— that you are about to put forward as an alternative to mine?

SOCRATES: No. I only want to subject yours to a critique. This is not a debate between two philosophies, only a cross-examination of one philosophy: yours.

KANT: All right, I will take your word for that. How then do you want to investigate this question of a possible self-contradiction that may be presupposed by my very question?

SOCRATES: I think we should not take any more time now to explore that possibility, since I want to get to what you have actually written, for that is our data, and we have already ignored that data for much too long. I have only meant to raise a doubt, not investigate it. But if you are interested in the doubt I have raised about this "critical question", the fundamental question of modern philosophy, and if you want to investigate it further, you might look up a conversation I had in this very place with Descartes a while ago. It was published in a book called *Socrates Meets Descartes*.

KANT: Descartes was here?

SOCRATES: Indeed he was.

KANT: Will I meet him?

SOCRATES: I think that is very probable. But that is not up to me.

KANT: You said there was a book about your conversation here with him. How would I get such a book in this place? I assume I cannot go back to earth.

SOCRATES: True. But in this place you can call up any book you want simply by willing it. For instance, there is *Socrates Meets Descartes* at your feet.

KANT: Oh. I see. But . . . how strange!—its pages will not open.

SOCRATES: They will open after we finish our conversation. I do not want it to prejudice your mind. There lies also *The Critique of Pure Reason* at your feet. You may pick it up and open to any page and you will see that it is indeed your book.

KANT: Oh! Are we going to examine that whole book?

SOCRATES: Oh, no. We will not subject *you* to the long mental tortures to which you subjected your readers.

Though that would be a just punishment for you, it would be an unjust sentence for anyone who might innocently find and read our little dialogue here.

KANT: This is more Socratic humor, I assume?

SOCRATES: You may assume that. Unless you are doing Descartes' new, modern, critical kind of philosophy, which assumes nothing.

KANT: I see. Your philosophy is so consistently ironic that you even make a joke out of your answer to the question: Was that a joke?

SOCRATES: I like to be consistent.

KANT: Will our conversation here be published in a book, like your conversation with Descartes?

SOCRATES: Yes. It will be entitled *Socrates Meets Kant*.

KANT: How is this possible?

SOCRATES: I will not answer that question now because it would distract us from our proper question, which is an investigation of your epistemology, and then an investigation of your ethics.

KANT: How will you examine my ethics?

SOCRATES: Not *I* but *we* will do it. We will examine it together, from the other book you now see at your feet.

KANT: It is the *Grounding for the Metaphysics of Morals*.

SOCRATES: Yes. And *that* little book we will examine much more carefully in a little while. But, first, we must turn back to your epistemology, and its origin in your personal history.

You were saying that you were dissatisfied with both modern philosophies, Rationalism and Empiricism, but that you were also dissatisfied with all premodern philosophies such as Plato's or Aristotle's or Aquinas' because they did not ask the critical question, the question of a justification of reason, the question of—if I may invent a very technical term—a "critique of pure reason".

KANT: This is so.

SOCRATES: Did you find anything else useful in the philosophy that began with Descartes?

KANT: Yes. In a word, the concentration on the human subject, and subjectivity.

SOCRATES: And you thought the ancients had neglected this?

KANT: Yes.

SOCRATES: And the moderns had not.

KANT: That's right. In fact all modern philosophers before me, insofar as they pointed to this subjective factor in knowledge, saw it as a *problem* for epistemology. The intrusion of the knowing subject between itself and the objective world seemed, to all of them, to *invalidate* knowledge and to *close* the way to certainty. My essential revolution was to question that assumption.

SOCRATES: So you might say that you made a virtue out of what to them was a vice.

KANT: In a sense, yes.

SOCRATES: *How* had they seen the intrusion of the knowing subject between itself and the objective world?

KANT: Bacon's notion of the "idols of the tribe", for one thing: those inevitable prejudices and false assumptions that the human mind cannot help making in all its attempts to know the objective world. For example, insisting that the world must be ordered in the same way as thought is ordered. This prejudice, Bacon thought, always led us to oversimplify reality.

Or Hume's notion of custom and habit as the real source of thinking in terms of causality. According to Hume, we think that the clouds *cause* the rain only because we have seen these two things in sequence many, many times, so the mental habit naturally arises in us of expecting the second thing whenever we see the first thing. So the purely mental causality within us—the custom of habituation that causes us to expect the second thing when we see the first thing— is projected out onto the things themselves, and we think the clouds really cause the rain. We think that the *clouds* cause the rain only because our *memory* of the clouds causes our *anticipation* of the rain.

SOCRATES: And what did you make of these suggestions in your epistemology?

KANT: In a word, I normalized this subjective intrusion. I showed how it is inevitable and necessary and natural to all human knowledge. And that was the essence of my "Copernican revolution in philosophy": the insight that the knowing mind is no longer a passive spectator, like a mirror, which simply reproduces the objective world when it knows, and which fails to know when it fails to passively reproduce the world. Instead, I said that the mind is an active creator in knowing, like an artist. Of course there *is* an objective world, as there *is* the artist's material. We do not create it. It is not mental; it is physical. But we shape our knowledge of it, as the artist shapes his material. He does not just copy it.

SOCRATES: This idea of yours, this "Copernican revolution", is indeed the central, and centrally original, and centrally radical, and centrally important, idea in your whole philosophy. For this reason, I hope you do not mind if we postpone a deeper investigation of it for now and first finish our investigation of the historical sources that led you to this revolutionary idea. For I think we will need more preliminaries than you have given us in the last few minutes if we are to fairly examine the idea.

KANT: I totally agree with you, Socrates. I would only point out that I proposed a similar and equally revolutionary idea in my ethics: that just as the mind is active in knowing, rather than passively receptive, so also the will is active in legislating the moral law rather than passively receiving it, as had previously been assumed.

SOCRATES: I thank you for so succinctly summarizing your two most important philosophical claims.

We now have the four following tasks before us, I think: first, to understand your fundamental epistemological idea, then to evaluate it, then to understand your fundamental ethical idea, and then to evaluate that.

KANT: Let us work in that logical order.

SOCRATES: In order to understand your first claim, the one in epistemology, we should first be sure we have finished our investigation of your historical sources. Do you wish to add anything to what you have already said about Rationalism and Empiricism?

KANT: Yes, I do. I have not yet explained how upsetting the philosophy of David Hume was to me, and how crucial this philosophical trauma was to the development of my thought.

SOCRATES: To that task, then, let us turn.

3

Haunted by Hume

KANT: Here is what I wrote:

I openly confess that my remembering David P 5
Hume was the very thing which many years
ago first interrupted my dogmatic slumber
and gave my investigations in the field of
speculative philosophy a quite new direction.
[For] **since the origin of metaphysics so far** P 2
as we know its history, nothing has ever hap-
pened which could have been more decisive
to its fate than the attack made upon it by
David Hume.

SOCRATES: What did you mean by "speculative" philosophy?

KANT: Metaphysics and epistemology as distinct from
ethics and aesthetics and politics. I wrote that human
reason asks three basic questions: CPR
                                                        B2
  1. **What can I know?**
  2. **What must I do?**
  3. **What may I hope?**

Speculative philosophy addresses the first question,
and its instrument is reason employed in the attempt

to know the truth simply for the sake of knowing it. This I called "pure reason", or "speculative reason".

Practical philosophy wants to know for the sake of acting and doing, and this I called "practical reason", or will.

The third question is harder to define. In fact it is not necessary to define it clearly in order to define the other two, so perhaps we should omit it here.

SOCRATES: Agreed. So it was Hume's attack on metaphysics that challenged you?

KANT: Yes, and the skepticism that it entailed. No one *wants* skepticism to be true. No one wants to believe that it is impossible for the human mind to know the universal principles and truths of objective reality, the real order of nature. But Hume seemed to prove that conclusion.

SOCRATES: Can you summarize just how Hume seemed to do this, without reviewing all the details of his argument?

KANT: Yes. It was essentially in two ways, I think. First there was his critique of metaphysics as uncritical because it was not based on experience and could not be proved or disproved by experience. And second, more specifically, there was his critique of causality.

SOCRATES: Did you agree with Hume's critique of metaphysics?

KANT: Of traditional metaphysics, yes. But not of all metaphysics. I would never have entitled my shorter version of *The Critique of Pure Reason* "*Prolegomena to Any Future Metaphysics*" if I had believed that.

SOCRATES: What mistake did you think you saw in Hume's critique of metaphysics, then?

KANT: I found in Hume a crucial ambiguity in the key term "experience". I thought Hume was quite right in insisting that experience is the necessary standard for proof or disproof of all the judgments of human reason. But I thought Hume unnecessarily limited experience to sense experience, or sensation.

SOCRATES: So you agreed with Hume's principle of not going beyond experience but you then tried to rehabilitate metaphysics by broadening the concept of experience so that it could be a basis for metaphysics—is that correct?

KANT: Yes.

SOCRATES: Was this your main concern, to rescue metaphysics from Hume?

KANT: To be totally honest, no. (I notice that it is impossible to lie in this place!)

It was science that was my primary concern. For not only did Hume write the death certificate for metaphysics, but also for science, even for Newtonian physics.

SOCRATES: How did he do that?

KANT: Through his critique of our knowledge of causality. He argued this way: All knowledge beyond present experience is based on the relation between cause and effect. And that is not what it seems to be:

it is not a law of objective nature but only a law of our own psychology.

SOCRATES: Why did he say that all knowledge beyond present experience is based on cause and effect?

KANT: Because experience shows this. For instance, if we receive a letter from a friend in another country, we see the letter and we reason to the friend as its cause even though we do not see him.

SOCRATES: So Hume's critique of this claim of reason —that it can go beyond experience via the principle of causality—was this what most specifically roused you from your dogmatic slumber?

KANT: Yes. As a disciple of the Rationalists I had un-thinkingly assumed that the principle of causality was a self-evident Cartesian "clear and distinct idea", and indubitable.

SOCRATES: Just *what* principle of causality did you mean?

KANT: It can be formulated very simply: that every event has a cause, or every change has a cause. This principle seems to be at the very heart of science, and even of all rational explanations of anything.

If something unusual happened—let's say a large rabbit suddenly appeared on my desk—I would never say, and no rational man would ever say, "Oh, well, rabbits just happen." We would assume it had a cause and then we would look for its cause.

We would first look for a natural physical cause: Did it fall through a hole in the ceiling? Did it hop up from the floor?

Then, if we were certain there was no physical cause, we would think there must be at least a mental cause, a hallucination or hypnosis.

And if this somehow turned out to be also impossible, then as a last resort we might think it may have had a supernatural cause and been a miracle. For even a miracle—if it really happens—has a cause. Even a miracle does not violate the principle of causality.

SOCRATES: All this sounds very reasonable to me.

KANT: As it did to me. I assumed that this principle of causality was an objective fact, a law of all nature, written into the nature of things. I also assumed that we knew its truth not by empirical observation, as we know that the sky is blue and the sun is bright, but by pure reason. Blind men would believe this principle just as readily as men with sight would.

SOCRATES: This all still sounds very reasonable. How did Hume make you doubt it?

KANT: He proved, or seemed to prove, that we could never know universal laws of nature by reason. We could know nature only by sense observation, and sense observation never reveals an absolutely universal law. "The sun rises every morning" is true so far in the history of our planet, but that does not prove it will rise tomorrow morning. No universal and necessary law can be proved by observation because what we observe with the senses is always the particular and the contingent.

SOCRATES: So Hume made you a skeptic?

KANT: About causality, yes. For a while, at least. He also pointed out that although we can observe *events that we label* causes, like a stick hitting a billiard ball, and though we can observe *events that we label effects*, like the billiard ball moving in the direction the stick pushed it, yet we cannot observe *causality itself*, or the causal *relation* itself. We see the stick move and the ball move but we do not see the transfer of force, or *the fact that* it is the stick as cause that moves the ball as effect.

SOCRATES: So did this make you just a skeptic of causality, or a *universal* skeptic?

KANT: To be a skeptic of causality *is* to be a universal skeptic, at least concerning our knowledge of nature. For as Hume pointed out, all our knowledge of nature that goes beyond our present sensation and memory of past sensation depends on the principle of causality.

SOCRATES: So how do we get the idea of causality, then, according to Hume, if it is not our reason's intuition of a real, universal, and necessary law of nature?

KANT: Hume reduced the principle of causality to mere habit or custom. It was purely psychological, purely subjective: when we see a thing happen many times, we expect it to happen again. That's all. The only causality we can know is between our memory and our anticipation, rather than between the events that we see.

SOCRATES: And did you become a skeptic because you accepted that explanation of Hume's?

KANT: No. I could not accept his skeptical conclusion.

SOCRATES: Why not?

KANT: Because if it is correct, then all Newtonian science is a fiction. All its discoveries of nature's inmost laws are merely our psychological expectations and habits. All natural science then is only psychology.

SOCRATES: Hmmm. . . . I wonder whether your "Copernican" solution to this problem will not result in that same absurd conclusion. No, no, I am going too fast.
  So would you say that your assumption was the validity of Newtonian science?

KANT: Well, yes, that was one assumption, at any rate.

SOCRATES: You did not regard that as controversial or in need of proof?

KANT: I regarded that as established.

SOCRATES: So Hume contradicted Newton, and as Newton was right, Hume was wrong somewhere.

KANT: It's not that simple, Socrates.

SOCRATES: Of course it's not that *simple*, but that was the logic of your thinking, however oversimplified, wasn't it?

KANT: Yes. That was my assumption: that Newtonian science was *actual*. And my philosophy explained how it was *possible*.

SOCRATES: Newtonian science depends on causality, does it not?

KANT: Indeed.

SOCRATES: How did you conclude that we do know causality, then? Did you go back to the Rationalists' explanation?

KANT: No, I couldn't do that. Hume had refuted that as dogmatic and uncritical. But since his refutation led to his skepticism even of science, that was equally unacceptable to me. So I had to find the error in both Rationalism and Empiricism. And here, I think, was my great original discovery:

At first I thought these two errors must be *opposite* errors, for they led to opposite conclusions that were wrong in opposite ways, the one not skeptical enough and the other too skeptical. But I came to see that there was a single common error, a single mistaken presupposition, that no one had ever noticed before. I unearthed, for the first time, I think, the hidden premise common to both the dogmatic Rationalist and the skeptical Empiricist. And once I found it, I denied that common premise. And that denial was *my* basic premise, my great new thought-experiment, my new "Copernican" hypothesis.

SOCRATES: So what, exactly, was that premise common to Descartes and Hume that you denied?

KANT: It was a premise common to *all* philosophers before me, including you, Socrates, and all your disciples: both Plato and Aristotle and all their medieval disciples, as well as modern Rationalists like Descartes and modern Empiricists like Hume. My denial of it was so revolutionary that I called that denial "the Copernican revolution in philosophy".

SOCRATES: Well, out with it, man! What was it?

KANT: As I wrote in the Preface to the second edition of my *Critique of Pure Reason*, **"Hitherto it has** CPR **been assumed that knowledge must conform to** Prol. **its objects."**

The assumption was that in order to work rightly, reason must reflect reality; that reason must intuit objectively real relations and principles and truths like causality and thus provide a kind of metaphysical map or X-ray of the nature of things. This assumption meant that when reason believes and uses the principle of causality, it is intellectually intuiting or seeing or mirroring the real nature of things as it exists before we know it and independent of our knowing it; that our knowing a thing does not change that thing, but that the thing changes our knowing.

SOCRATES: You denied that there is any such thing as intellectual intuition, then?

KANT: Yes. There is only sensory intuition of particulars, not intellectual intuition of universals. We do not "see" Platonic forms with our minds as we see colors and shapes with our eyes.

SOCRATES: But that denial is not new. It is the teaching of William of Ockham in the late Middle Ages. It is part of his doctrine of Nominalism: that universals (such as causality, or justice, or human nature, or any other universals) are not objectively real but only subjectively, artificially invented "nomina" or names. According to Nominalism, we do not intuit them, we invent them. If that's all you meant by your "Copernican revolution", it seems that you claimed to be more revolutionary than you actually were.

KANT: No, that's not all I meant.

SOCRATES: What more, then, did you mean?

KANT: As Copernicus changed the absolute in astronomy, I changed the absolute in philosophy. Instead of the sun being relative to the earth, in revolving around the earth, Copernicus said the earth is relative to the sun and revolves around the sun. The sun only *appears* to move—to rise and set. Really it is we who are moving.

SOCRATES: And how is this revolution in astronomy parallel to your revolution in philosophy?

KANT: Thinking universal principles is like observing the motion of the sun. When we think universal principles like causality, it seems that this comes from without, from nature; it seems that we see it, we reflect it, we mirror an objective *logos*, a rational order in nature. But this is not so. It appears that way, but it is not really that way. Really, all the order comes from us. In the act of knowing, the subject of knowing determines, forms, shapes, or structures the object of knowing, not vice versa, as everyone had thought. That is my "Copernican revolution".

SOCRATES: I see. That is indeed revolutionary. We will examine its credentials shortly. Meanwhile, how did this new idea of yours answer Hume?

KANT: Hume asked how we could know that every event must have a cause before we had experienced every event. And his only answer was that we *couldn't* know it. It was just a nonrational habit, a custom; it was not part of *reason*.

SOCRATES: And you showed how it *was* part of reason?

KANT: Yes: by redefining reason, or reason's job. Reason's job was not to mirror the nature of things but to *construct* the nature of things, as an artist constructs his art: not to *discover* the form in the matter and abstract it into a universal principle, but to *put* the form in the matter, to impose the form on the matter as a sculptor imposes shape on marble, or a musician imposes melody on sound.

SOCRATES: I think I see. Test me: see whether I am understanding your relationship to Hume correctly.

Hume came to his skeptical conclusions only because he believed two premises, one overt and one hidden.

The *overt* premise was that reason cannot know the principle of causality, or any other universal and necessary principles that were objectively true, or "matters of fact" as distinct from mere "relations of ideas" like $2 + 2 = 4$ or "bachelors are unmarried".

The *hidden* premise was that reason was *supposed* to know these things, that reason's job was to mirror the structure of reality.

If reason was supposed to mirror the universal structures of reality, and if reason could not mirror the universal structures of reality, then reason is a failure and we must be skeptics. But if reason is not *supposed* to passively mirror and discover and receive structures and forms and principles from reality, but rather its job is to create those forms, as your "Copernican revolution" suggests, then reason is doing its job quite well and we need not be skeptics about reason. Thus you have done a critique of reason, as Hume has—that is, you have asked the critical question, as Hume has—but you have also defended reason and rescued it from Humean skepticism.

KANT: That is precisely what I did. Thank you for putting it so simply and logically, Socrates.

But I did not regard Hume as simply my opponent to be refuted, but as my helper, to be used. Hume was not all wrong. In fact, his fundamental point, his critique of Rationalism, was right. Hume corrected Rationalism by pointing out that all our knowledge of "matters of fact", as distinct from "relations of ideas", had to be verified by experience. That was one of his premises: the correct one. But he also assumed an incorrect one. And that was that experience was mere sense experience. As an Empiricist, he reduced experience to sensation and said that all concepts are merely pale copies of percepts. That was his error.

SOCRATES: I should think *that* critique would be fairly obvious for anyone who is not an Empiricist. It amounts to little more than disagreeing with Empiricism.

KANT: Oh, no, Socrates, it is much more than that. My critique of Hume was much more technical than just that. In fact I had to invent a new system of technical terminology to express it. I said that the principle of causality was an example of a "synthetic a priori proposition". And what I meant by that was . . .

SOCRATES: I'm afraid I need to interrupt you here. Let's postpone the technical terminology for our next conversation.

KANT: As you say, Socrates. What do you want to investigate now, then?

SOCRATES: I just want to raise one question now. If we accept this analysis of the argument—that Hume's skepticism rested on his two premises, and that one of these two premises had to be denied if we are to avoid his skeptical conclusion—why did you not deny his other premise, the overt one, the Nominalist one? That's what most of the philosophers of ancient and medieval times did: Plato, and Aristotle, and Augustine, and Aquinas. . . .

KANT: I thought that was just uncritical, Socrates.

SOCRATES: But if skepticism is false, and if it depends on the Nominalist premise, does that not show that the Nominalist premise is false? Isn't that a critical, logical argument that raises the critical question of skepticism and then answers it? Doesn't that critically refute skepticism?

KANT: That is not the kind of critique I offered. That is a purely abstract logical argument. It does not explain how knowledge actually works.

SOCRATES: No, it does not. But there are philosophers who do: philosophers like Plato, with his theory of Recollection, and Aristotle and Aquinas with their theory of abstraction, and Augustine, with his theory of Divine Illumination. Perhaps one of them is correct. Why did you not consider them and refute them first before casting about for a new and revolutionary epistemology?

KANT: As I have already told you, Socrates, they were premodern and uncritical. They did not begin with a critique of reason.

SOCRATES: Why did you assume that we had to begin with a critique of reason?

KANT: Because once the question was raised, by Descartes—once Descartes began with universal doubt and doubted reason itself—this question could no longer be ignored but had to be answered.

SOCRATES: Suppose the question *cannot* be answered? Suppose there is, as I suggested in our previous conversation, a logical contradiction inherent in the demand for a rational justification of reason itself?

KANT: If that is so, I would not know where to turn, except to turn to faith—either religious faith in God as the creator and designer of human reason or to a merely human faith in reason itself. But faith cannot be proved. And if it could be proved, I would have to prove it by reason. But if I did that, I would again be caught in the logical contradiction of giving a rational proof of reason itself, for I would then be first giving a rational justification for faith and then putting forward faith (either human or divine) as the justification for reason. That would be a circular argument.

SOCRATES: It would indeed. And does that not seem to show that there is something wrong with the question itself, if all possible answers to it involve something as illogical as that?

KANT: But are you suggesting that philosophers should simply ignore the critical question?

SOCRATES: Is that what I have been doing here?

KANT: No. . . .

SOCRATES: What have I been doing?

KANT: You have been criticizing the critical question.

SOCRATES: As you did not do.

KANT: True.

SOCRATES: Which of us, then, is the more critical thinker, and which of us is the more naïve?

KANT: You turn everything upside down, Socrates.

SOCRATES: Yes. Perhaps that is because I am standing on my head. But, on the other hand, that might be because *you* are.

KANT: I do not wish to argue by means of metaphors, Socrates, and I am disappointed in you that you would do so.

SOCRATES: I am not arguing in metaphors, Immanuel, because I am not arguing at all. I am merely raising a question for you that you seem not to have raised for yourself.

KANT: What question?

SOCRATES: You raised the question of the critique of reason. I raise the question of the critique of the critique. You called your book *The Critique of Pure Reason*, but I wonder whether you ever turned your formidable critical powers on yourself.

KANT: I see what you are doing.

SOCRATES: Do you say that is a fair question, or not? Shouldn't a philosophy be able to account for itself by its own methods?

KANT: Of course. But that was not the purpose of my book. And I thought we were here to discuss that book, *The Critique of Pure Reason*, and not another book, the book that you imply I should have written but did not, namely, *The Critique of The Critique of Pure Reason.*

SOCRATES: You are quite right. Let us now turn to the book you have written.

4

The Fundamental Question of
The Critique of Pure Reason

SOCRATES: Any book of philosophy, it seems to me, seeks to give its reader answers. Would you not agree?

KANT: True.

SOCRATES: And answers are answers to questions.

KANT: Of course.

SOCRATES: So if we do not understand the question that is being asked, we will not understand the answer to it, even if we understand every word in the answer. We will be like spectators at a military battle who arrive late in the day, after one army has launched an all-out attack in the center, which we have not seen. We will then wonder why the second army, which is stronger and wiser than the first, and which is destined to win the day's battle, seems to be in retreat in the center, instead of bringing up reinforcements there, and why it is instead reinforcing its wings, even though the wings are not being attacked. The reason, of course, is that the second army is luring the first into being surrounded.

KANT: An apt metaphor, Socrates. Is it also an allegory? Do you say this explains my strategy point by point?

SOCRATES: No. I give you this illustration only to show that even if you understand *what* is happening, whether on a battlefield or in an argument, you may not understand *why*. So we must take some more time to understand your question before we can rightly understand your revolutionary answer to it.

KANT: I completely agree with your principle. But I thought we had already explored my question, in tracing my problem to my predecessors, especially Descartes' raising the "critical question" of justifying human reason, and Hume's Empiricism rousing me from my "dogmatic slumber" of Rationalism by apparently refuting it and putting in its place a theory of knowledge that necessarily resulted in skepticism, especially skepticism of Newtonian science.

SOCRATES: That was the broader historical question *outside* your book, which explained why you had to write the book. But now we should explore the specific logical question *inside* your book, the question the book itself claims to answer.

KANT: I agree completely with your procedure.

SOCRATES: Then what was that question? Or was it more than one question? If only one, it is remarkable that it took such a long and difficult book to answer it. For the single question you put to yourself in *Grounding for the Metaphysics of Morals* took only a very short and relatively simple book to answer.

KANT: It was only one question, but we could express it in two ways. In the broadest sense, my question was: How is human knowledge possible? Assuming knowledge is actual, what makes it possible? What are the conditions of its possibility, or its preconditions? That is what I meant by calling it a "transcendental" critique of reason.

SOCRATES: Is that all you meant by the term "transcendental"? Most people, when they hear the word "transcendental", think "supernatural".

KANT: That is not what I meant at all. I distinguished the "transcendental" from the "transcendent". By the "transcendental" I meant transcending human experience in the subjective direction, asking: What is it in us, or in reason, that makes possible the knowledge that we actually have? By the "transcendent" I meant transcending human experience in the objective direction, asking: What is there in objective reality that is independent of our experience of it, that thus "transcends" experience? I called the second question impossible to answer, but the first question possible. And my *Critique* was my attempt to answer that first question.

SOCRATES: I see. And what was the other, less broad way of expressing the question of your book?

KANT: "How are a priori synthetic judgments possible?"

SOCRATES: Obviously we need some definitions of terms.

KANT: Of course. A "judgment" is the act of the mind that is expressed in a proposition, a declarative sentence that can be true (or false) and can constitute knowledge.

SOCRATES: That's clear.

KANT: Now Hume had divided all judgments into *only two kinds*: "matters of fact" and "relations of ideas".

"Matters of fact" for Hume were judgments like "the sky is blue" or "the sun will rise tomorrow" or "most married men live longer than bachelors". They add to our knowledge. They give us information. Their predicates add something to their subjects that is not already contained in the idea of the subject. And for this reason we need sense experience to know that they are true. There is no innate idea of the sky being blue or the sun rising tomorrow.

"Relations of ideas", on the other hand, for Hume, were judgments like "X does not equal non-X" or "All rational animals are animals" or "No impossible thing is possible." We do not need any experience to know that they are true, but they do not give us any information about the world, because their predicates do not add anything to their subjects.

SOCRATES: That seems quite clear. Did you accept or reject this classification of judgments that you found in Hume?

KANT: I rejected it. For it classified judgments by two different standards at once. One standard was epistemological: How do we know the judgment is true? How do we find out? Is it by sense experience or by pure reason? Do we look at the world or at the idea? The other standard was logical: Within the logical structure of the judgment itself, does the predicate add any intelligible meaning to the subject, or not?

So I distinguished those two different questions. As to the question of how we know the judgment is true, I called judgments that are arrived at by sense experience "a posteriori judgments". "A posteriori" means "posterior to, or after"—posterior to sense experience. And I called judgments that we know to be true even prior to sense experience "a priori" judgments.

Then I added a second distinction, based on a second question, which is about something intrinsic to the judgment itself rather than how we know it, something in the logical structure of the judgment. If the meaning of the predicate is already contained within the meaning of the subject, I call it an "analytic" judgment, for its predicate only "analyzes" the meaning, or part of the meaning, of the subject.

In contrast, any judgment that is informative, that is, whose predicate adds new meaning to its subject that is not already contained within the essential meaning, or concept, or essence, or definition, of the subject itself, I called a "synthetic" judgment. It "synthesizes", or joins, a subject and a predicate, as marriage joins a man and a woman, who are different.

SOCRATES: In heterosexual marriage, anyway.

KANT: Is there another kind?

SOCRATES: That is one of the controversial issues that Western civilization will argue about centuries after your time, Immanuel.

KANT: So they will argue over whether the proposition "marriage is heterosexual" is an analytic or synthetic proposition?

SOCRATES: Well, now, I think that both sides of that controversy would claim that it is not about propositions but about real people, and real marriage, and real gender. Most people who are not philosophers think more about real things than about the propositions that express them, you know.

KANT: Ah, yes. So I have noticed.

SOCRATES: Do I detect in the sigh that accompanies your words some note of pity or regret?—that ordinary people are not philosophers?

KANT: No, Socrates, it was merely my pitiful attempt at humor. I am fully aware that *whomever* we can marry, we cannot marry propositions.

SOCRATES: I accept your attempt at humor. I will not explore the question of whether I can accept society's new classification of marriages, but I *will* explore whether I can accept your new classification of propositions.

We have four possible kinds of judgments, by your classification, rather than only two, as Hume said. Is that correct?

KANT: Four that are logically possible, yes. But we find only three that are actual if we explore the whole range of human knowledge.

There are no a posteriori judgments that are also analytic. For if they were analytic, we would know them a priori, before experience, simply by analyzing the meaning of the terms. We need a posteriori experience only for synthetic judgments, judgments whose predicate adds new meaning to the subject that cannot be analyzed out of the subject.

Judgments that are a priori and analytic are what Hume called "relations of ideas".

Judgments that are a posteriori and synthetic are what Hume called "matters of fact".

But we also find some judgments that are synthetic and a priori. And these Hume could not account for. I can. That is the claim of my *Critique*.

SOCRATES: Give me some examples of judgments that are both synthetic and a priori.

KANT: I will give you four kinds of synthetic a priori judgments.

My first example may be a bit tricky and controversial. It will certainly be surprising, to anyone who has read Hume. All the propositions of *mathematics*, I believe, are a priori, but also synthetic rather than analytic—the propositions in Euclid's geometry, for instance.

Second, all universal principles in *science* are synthetic and a priori, such as the Uniformity of Nature, or the Principle of Causality, that "every event has a cause". Also included are the more specific principles of Newtonian physics, such as the principle that force equals mass multiplied by acceleration. For this truth is universal and necessary, and we can know with certainty that it will be true tomorrow, as we do *not* know with certainty, but only with probability, that the sun will rise tomorrow. Since no one denies the success of Newtonian physics, this is the most useful of the four kinds of a priori synthetic judgments to explore, for here we have universally admitted data. There *are* a priori synthetic judgments. My question is not whether they exist but why—not whether they are actual but how they are possible.

Third, all the principles of *metaphysics* are synthetic and a priori, such as "God exists" or "Matter and spirit are distinct substances" or "Wills are free" or "Souls are immortal." Now some will say, with

Hume, that metaphysics is simply impossible, that it is a fake, that we must be skeptical of all metaphysics. I do not say that, though I do say that traditional metaphysics, before Hume, was mistaken, and uncritical, and dogmatic, and I offer a new kind of metaphysics, one that is transcendental rather than transcendent.

Fourth, the fundamental principles of *morality* are synthetic and a priori. These, however, are not expressed in declarative sentences but in imperatives, such as "Treat others as you will that they treat you", or "Do not use others as means but respect them as ends." So you might want to say that they do not really constitute *knowledge*. For they do not tell you what *is* but only what *ought* to be. Traditional moral philosophers before Hume believed that they did constitute knowledge of what-is: for instance, that "there *is* a natural moral law", or that "the greatest good *is* happiness", or that "to do justice *is* a moral obligation."

Now I foresee that my first kind of a priori synthetic propositions will be controversial, since the disciples of Hume will classify the propositions of mathematics as analytical, which I do not do. But the most controversial kind will be the fourth kind. For the opponents of Hume who believe in a "natural law" morality, the traditionalists, will classify moral imperatives as propositions that give us knowledge, that inform us about being, about what-is; and I am reluctant to admit that. For that confuses imperative with declarative sentences. The disciples of Hume, on the other hand, will classify moral propositions as mere conventions or expressions of emotion. They will make an absolute distinction between "facts" and "values", and they will say that values are purely subjective expressions of feeling—and I am even more reluctant to agree with that.

So perhaps we should argue about those two classes or propositions later and concentrate at first only on the remaining two kinds, the less controversial ones, the propositions of natural science and metaphysics.

SOCRATES: I think that is a wise strategy. But I find it interesting and ironic that you will be criticized for being insufficiently Humean regarding your first class of propositions and too Humean regarding your fourth class. I suppose that's just Humean nature.

KANT: (Silence).

SOCRATES: It was a very bad pun, I grant you, and it deserved your silent rebuke.

KANT: Since you now understand my question—how are synthetic a priori judgments possible?—I think it is time to explore my answer.

SOCRATES: Let us not be too hasty. Are we not being too uncritical in not questioning one very obvious assumption that you make in your fourfold classification of judgments?

KANT: Oh, you mean the assumption that a priori synthetic judgments are actual? That is indeed an assumption that Hume would question. But I think the example of Newton's physics has established that assumption without doubt, even if my other three classes of a priori synthetic propositions are questionable.

SOCRATES: No, I was not thinking of that assumption. I was thinking of your assumption that there is no fourth kind of proposition.

KANT: Analytic a posteriori propositions? But if a proposition is analytic, we know it to be true simply by analyzing its meaning. We know it a priori. Why would we seek to confirm it a posteriori, by sense experience?

SOCRATES: You yourself said that Hume was wrong in reducing experience to sense experience only. Perhaps we learn such analytic truths as "every event has a cause" by experience after all, though not merely sense experience.

KANT: I do not see how that is possible. For a priori propositions are universally true only because they are logically necessary, on pain of contradiction. If you deny them, you contradict yourself, since their predicates are already contained in their subjects, and merely analyzed out of their subjects. Thus "all rational animals are animals" is not learned from experience or proved by experience, any more than "all two-headed extraterrestrials are extraterrestrials."

SOCRATES: Some of these propositions are about unreal objects, like two-headed extraterrestrials, while others are about real objects, like rational animals. Isn't that so?

KANT: Yes.

SOCRATES: Might it not be that we learn about real objects from experiencing them? Especially if experience is not limited to sense experience?

KANT: Of course that is possible. But are you suggesting that the *universality and necessity* that distin-

guishes analytic propositions can be derived from experience? How could that be?

SOCRATES: It might be that universal and necessary
forms are embedded in matter, in material substances,
and are derived from our experience of these substances by a process of abstraction, as Aristotle and
Aquinas say.

KANT: What do you mean by "forms"? Structures?
Shapes? Those are sensory.

SOCRATES: No, I mean what the medievals called
essences, natures, whatnesses, or quiddities, answers
to the question "quid est?" "*What* is it?"

KANT: That is a most primitive and uncritical notion.

SOCRATES: But it is the fundamental notion in all of
philosophy, if Plato is right. And my famous "Socratic method"—my method of demanding a logically consistent and experientially accurate definition
of such things as "justice" or "piety" or "death" or
"love" and arguing until we found one—the whole
point of this method was to find such forms. There
are many other words for it besides "form". The ancients called it the *logos*, the "word" or intelligibility
or reason or design or structure or meaning inherent
in the thing, not just in the word or the concept. It
is the alternative to Nominalism, which reduces all
such universal forms to mere words.

KANT: But this old philosophy uncritically assumes
two things: in metaphysics, a realism of universals
rather than a Nominalism that denies them, and

in epistemology a real intellectual intuition of these essences or universals.

SOCRATES: In other words, intelligibility and intellection. Yes, this is true. Ancient philosophers did usually make those two assumptions. And you do not, I think. Is that true?

KANT: Yes.

SOCRATES: So you are a Nominalist, then? You deny real universals?

KANT: No. That is a question about metaphysics. I deny the possibility of traditional metaphysics, "transcendent" metaphysics.

SOCRATES: But you do deny the existence of any "intellectual intuition" in your *Critique*, do you not?

CPR
B75
A51

KANT: Yes. I claim that **"The understanding intuits nothing, but only reflects."** Intuition is sensory, not intellectual.

SOCRATES: And the objects of intellectual intuition are universals, are they not?

KANT: Yes. I deny that we can begin with the two uncritical assumptions of intuition and universals, as Plato and Aristotle did.

SOCRATES: But aren't your two denials just as much uncritical *assumptions*—rather than conclusions—as Plato's or Aristotle's opposite assumptions? Even more uncritical, it seems, for you did not even consider the *possibility* of the existence of a posteriori analytic judgments, which would contradict these assumptions. So you would seem to be *less* critical than the ancients.

KANT: No, more. Much more. For I raised "the critical question", as they did not: the question of the justification of human knowledge.

SOCRATES: That is true. But suppose it turns out, upon analysis, as I have suggested before, that "the critical question" is logically unanswerable? Or suppose it turns out that the only possible answer to it turns out to have hidden assumptions that are just as questionable as the assumptions of the ancients? Suppose that these assumptions are even more questionable? Suppose they are logically self-contradictory?

KANT: You have not proved any one of these suppositions, Socrates.

SOCRATES: Of course not. I am only asking you the question What if? What if our investigation should show any one of these things, or all of them? What would this show about your *Critique*?

KANT: It would certainly raise critical questions about it. I think I could answer those questions, Socrates. But I do not think that an honest investigation of my book will lead to any of those results. Do you claim to know that it will? Do you claim to know that already, even before we begin?

SOCRATES: No. My only critique of your critique so far is that it is not critical enough, that you have left some relevant questions unraised in the very process of raising your so-called "critical question".

KANT: I do not accept your characterization of my philosophy as more uncritical than yours.

SOCRATES: Come, now, Immanuel, you know me better than that. I am not defending "my" philosophy. In fact, I have little or no philosophy to defend. My job is not to lecture but to question. I am your intellectual psychoanalyst.

KANT: All right, then, but in arguing against me you are arguing for Rationalism.

SOCRATES: No, I am not arguing for anything. I am only critiquing your *Critique*. And surely not all philosophers who disagree with you are Rationalists. Even Plato was not a Rationalist in the same way that Descartes and Spinoza and Leibniz were. And Aristotle was not a Rationalist at all.

KANT: But this notion of *logos*, or essences, or forms —surely it is the hallmark of a philosophy that is naïve and uncritical. You can't even specify what it means, much less prove it.

SOCRATES: I think I *can* specify what it means, if given a chance. Would you like me to explain the *metaphysical* notion of forms or the *epistemological* notion of how we know forms? (Please keep in mind that I am *not* assuming this old philosophy to be true. I am just putting it forward as a possible alternative to yours, an alternative that you seem not to have considered.)

KANT: I would like you to explain the epistemological notion, please.

SOCRATES: Very well. According to Aristotle and Aquinas, we abstract the common universal form from the particular individuating matter. We abstract treeness from trees, or justice from just men and just acts and just laws.

KANT: You reason from the particular to the universal, then. This is inductive reasoning. It is generalization. And inductive reasoning is only probable, not certain. So it is very uncritical to rest all of philosophy on this foundation!

SOCRATES: No, it is not inductive reasoning because it is not reasoning at all. "Abstraction" comes under what the medievals called the "first act of the mind", conceiving a concept, which is not expressed in a proposition at all but only in a term, a subject or a predicate. Abstraction comes *before* the "second act of the mind", which is judgment, judging a predicate to be true of a subject. And it certainly comes before the "third act of the mind", reasoning from some judgments to others, from premises to a conclusion, whether inductively or deductively.

KANT: Well, how does abstraction of the universal form work? You just "see" it?

SOCRATES: I think it is something like a hunter entering a jungle to find a tiger. The hunter is the mind, the jungle is reality, or the world, and the tiger is the universal form. As the tiger lives in the jungle, the universal form exists in its particular substances. Justice exists in just people, acts, societies, and laws, and human nature exists in human beings, and greenness exists in green things.

Now let us suppose the hunter does not want to kill the tiger but just take it captive. He will shoot it with a drug that paralyzes and immobilizes it. Then he will take it out of the jungle and put it into a cage in a city zoo. Similarly, the mind abstracts the universal, which is unchanging and immobile, from the changing concrete things where it actually lives, so to speak, and cages it in a concept. It puts its prey into the mental realm, like the city zoo, which is full of other caged concepts, because there in its immobile cage it can be studied objectively and accurately and compared with the other caged animals, the other universal forms.

KANT: Does this philosophy claim that minds *make* concepts?

SOCRATES: No. As zoos cannot create tigers, minds cannot create forms, only receive them from the jungles of the world through the actions of hunters, which are mental acts. And when the mind receives a form into itself, that form in the mind is called a concept.

KANT: I see. So if we were speaking of reasoning here (what you called "the third act of the mind"), you would say that deduction receives all its data from induction.

SOCRATES: If I were defending this philosophy— which is essentially Aristotle's, not Plato's—then yes, I would say that. And I would say that deduction *must* depend on induction because no syllogism can prove its own premises without begging the question. And the process of proving the premises of any deductive argument will just go on and on forever—we must prove the premises of the new argument that proves the premises of the first one, and so on. And then no premise will be certain, and thus no conclusion certain either, unless we get our first premises by induction rather than deduction.

KANT: So abstraction in the "first act of the mind" is like induction in the "third act of the mind"? They function in parallel ways?

SOCRATES: Yes. They both rise from the particular to the universal.

KANT: Perhaps I should consider this possibility more carefully. I thought there were only two alternatives, Rationalism and Empiricism, and I tried to reconcile them and build a bridge between reason and experience. And my bridge was a new one, in fact a revolutionary one. But there also seems to be an old bridge already built long before me, from ancient times. Whether this old bridge holds the weight of the traffic of human knowledge as well as mine does, however, is another question.

SOCRATES: Still, I wonder why you did not explore and refute those ancient alternatives more explicitly, the alternative hypotheses to your "Copernican" one. You must have known that there were indeed other options, both in metaphysics and in epistemology. And you must have known that each of these options contains both a metaphysic and an epistemology, a metaphysics to fit each epistemology and an epistemology to fit each metaphysic.

KANT: You speak of a plurality of ancient options. What are they? How do you classify these options?

SOCRATES: Why, in a very simple-minded way, I think —a way that is shown both by the inner logic of the question and by the history of philosophical answers to them.

In metaphysics, there is Plato's "extreme realism", Aristotle's "moderate realism", Ockham's Nominalism, and Gorgias' Nihilism. All four are answers to the question of universals, or *logos*.

Plato says that universals like roundness or humanity exist in themselves independently and are more real than individual round things or human beings.

Aristotle says that they are objectively real but not separate from things: they are the forms of things. Roundness is in round things and humanity in human beings.

Ockham says they are only words, only our meaningful and useful names, but are not objectively real.

And Gorgias says they are not even meaningful names. There is no *logos*.

KANT: And what are the four epistemologies that you say correspond to these four metaphysics?

SOCRATES: First, there is Plato's Rationalism, which claims to have a direct intellectual intuition of the Ideas. Descartes fits that pattern also, I think.

Second, there is Aristotle's Moderate Empiricism, which claims that our knowledge begins with sense experience but does not end there because we can then abstract the universal forms from particular matter.

Third, there is Hume's Extreme Empiricism, which claims that our knowledge is limited to sense experience of particulars.

And fourth, there is simple Skepticism.

KANT: But I am not a Humean Empiricist. In a way I am the closest to Aristotle, because I too believe that, as I wrote, **"all our knowledge begins with experience. It does not follow, however, that it is limited to experience."** I too tried to combine reason and sensation. But I have invented a fifth epistemology, which does not fit into any one of your four. CPR B1

SOCRATES: I think you have indeed. But why did you think that was necessary?

KANT: Because I believed that there are more serious difficulties in all four other epistemologies than in mine. But I would love to have the opportunity to dialogue with Plato about this. Could you arrange that, Socrates?

SOCRATES: Some other time, perhaps.

KANT: Is Plato here?

SOCRATES: He is. I had the occasion to cross-examine him at length about his *Republic*. But we are not here to investigate his philosophy today but rather yours. So let us turn back to your book now. We have explored your question; now let us explore your answer.

5

Kant's Big Idea: His "Copernican Revolution" in Philosophy

SOCRATES: This will surely be our most important conversation, and therefore probably our longest. For we are now ready to focus on your most famous, central, and most revolutionary idea, your "Copernican revolution in philosophy". Indeed, it seems to be one of the most revolutionary ideas in the entire history of human thought.

How do you think we should investigate this key idea? What questions should we ask about it?

KANT: To be logically complete, I think we must examine this idea from three points of view, Socrates.

First, what is the idea? What does it mean? Define it.

Second, how did I arrive at it? What is my logical path to it, my argument for it?

Third, what are the logical consequences, or corollaries of this idea? Just how revolutionary is it? What are the consequences of this revolution? So we should look at the thing itself, its causes, and its effects.

SOCRATES: I agree that these three questions are necessary, but I think you left out the most important one of all.

KANT: What's that?

SOCRATES: Is it true?

KANT: Oh. Well . . .

SOCRATES: Is truth an afterthought to you?

KANT: Certainly not.

SOCRATES: What is the problem then?

KANT: One of the consequences of my new idea is that our idea of truth itself is revolutionized.

SOCRATES: In that case, it may be tricky, or even self-contradictory, to argue that the idea is "true" or "false" in the old sense, when the idea itself gives "truth" a new sense. Could we define the old sense of "truth", to start with?

KANT: That is easy. Old Aristotle defined truth simply as thinking and saying what is, the mind mirroring reality, the content of thinking reproducing the content of being.

That was his so-called realist epistemology.

SOCRATES: And your new idea cannot be classified under this old one, can it?

KANT: No, for the whole point of my revolutionary new idea is that Aristotle was wrong.

SOCRATES: How?

KANT: Aristotle confused the mirror and the thing mirrored. For my idea is that reality mirrors thought rather than vice versa.

SOCRATES: Are you speaking here of divine thought, the thought of the Creator and Designer of nature, or of human thought? For the idea that the reality of nature mirrors the thought of the Creator and Designer of it does not seem to be a new or revolutionary thought at all.

KANT: No, I speak only of human thought. My philosophy is more modest than to claim to know the mind of God.

SOCRATES: So you are merely mapping human thought.

KANT: Yes.

SOCRATES: "Mapping" something is pretty much the same thing as "mirroring" it, isn't it?

KANT: Yes.

SOCRATES: I wonder how you can do that, then, if your "Copernican revolution" denies that thought does map or mirror reality. That seems to be an inherent self-contradiction.

KANT: I will address the charge of inherent self-contradiction, if you wish. But before I do, I must retract a slip of the tongue in characterizing my philosophy. It is *not* an attempt to map human thought. That is what psychology and anthropology do, in different ways. My epistemology is more ambitious than that. It attempts to do more than merely to describe the human mind as part of human nature.

SOCRATES: A moment ago you said it was *not* so ambitious as to claim to describe the *divine* mind. Now you say it is *more* ambitious than merely to claim to describe the *human* mind. What mind do you speak of, then? The mind of an angel?

KANT: No, the mind of man. But I do not merely describe human thought as determined by *human nature*. I do not claim to know human nature as a thing-in-itself. I do not give you an anthropology, a science of human nature, or of human reason as determined by human nature.

SOCRATES: What then do you give us?

KANT: A science of reason itself, reason as such. I think I have discovered the innate forms of all rational thought.

SOCRATES: Not just *human* rational thought?

KANT: No. If there are rational beings of very different kinds on other planets, they too must think in these essential ways, the ways that I have discovered and mapped, if they are to think rationally at all.

SOCRATES: Well, of course they must. The laws of logic are not so narrow that they cease to hold when one moves from Greece to Germany, or even from Earth to Mars. That idea is hardly revolutionary.

KANT: Oh, but I mean much more than the laws of logic, Socrates. I mean three different ways in which reason structures the objects of our thought. I call them the "forms of perception", the "categories", and the "ideas of Pure Reason". They are like three layers of the cake of my "Copernican revolution".

SOCRATES: But before we go into detail about the three layers of your revolutionary "Copernican" cake, I think we should investigate its essential core. We should understand your "big idea" before investigating the smaller ones.

KANT: Fine. How do you propose to do that?

SOCRATES: What better way than by beginning with the memorable and oft-quoted passage from your Preface to the second edition of the *Critique of Pure Reason*. Would you read it, please, and explain it as you go along?

KANT: What a strange and wonderful place this is! As soon as I formulated my wish to see that passage, the book leaped up into my hand and opened itself to the passage I wanted. Is this the place where dreams and desires come true?

SOCRATES: Yes—and in ways you may not have dreamed of.

KANT: And also nightmares and fears?

SOCRATES: I will not answer that question now.

KANT: Why?

SOCRATES: Because it is a distraction.

KANT: I accept your authority in this place.

SOCRATES: Then please read the passage so that we can investigate it further.

KANT: (reading)

CPR
xvi

Hitherto it has been assumed that all our knowledge must conform to objects. But all attempts to extend our knowledge of objects by establishing something in regard to them *a priori*, by means of concepts [in other words, what I call synthetic a priori knowledge] **have, on this assumption, ended in failure.**

[This was the failure exposed by Hume.] **We must therefore make trial whether we may not have more success in the tasks of metaphysics if we suppose that objects must conform to our knowledge. This would agree better with what is desired, namely, that it should be possible to have knowledge of objects *a priori*, determining something in regard to them prior to their being given.** [In other words, this would explain how we have synthetic a priori knowledge.] **We should then be proceeding precisely on the lines of Copernicus' primary hypothesis. Failing of satisfactory progress in explaining the movements of the heavenly bodies on the supposition that they all revolve around the spectator, he tried whether he might not have more success if he made the spectator to revolve and the stars to remain at rest.**

SOCRATES: Here we have a truly revolutionary suggestion, one of the most crucial turning points in the history of human thought.

KANT: I thank you for the compliment, Socrates.

SOCRATES: I did not mean it as a compliment.

KANT: Did you mean it as an insult, then?

SOCRATES: No. You see, I seem to have this strange habit: I like to describe an idea, and understand it, before I evaluate it, so that I know just what it is that I am evaluating.

KANT: You are being sarcastic.

SOCRATES: Yes. And I am also being sarcastic when I say that I do not tell the truth with a calendar.

KANT: What do you mean by that?

SOCRATES: I mean that I do not assume that just because an idea is revolutionary it must be true, as so-called Progressives tend to do, *or* that it is false, as so-called Conservatives tend to do.

KANT: Neither do I.

SOCRATES: Good. Then we will not cheat.

KANT: What do you mean by that?

SOCRATES: I mean that we will investigate the idea itself rather than its age or its parentage.

KANT: I agree.

SOCRATES: Then let us begin.

KANT: I have a suggestion for you, Socrates, but I fear it may appear strange to you.

SOCRATES: What is that?

KANT: I suggest that it might be helpful if you would actually begin instead of repeatedly exhorting us to begin.

SOCRATES: Oh, Immanuel, you do have a sense of humor after all. How delightful! Well, then, my first question is an obvious one. It seems that your new idea is not like the Copernican revolution at all, but the exact opposite of it.

KANT: How do you mean?

SOCRATES: In a word, Copernicus objectivized the absolute whereas you subjectivize it.

KANT: What do you mean by that?

SOCRATES: Copernicus said that the astronomical absolute was not the earth but the sun, and that the motion of the earth was relative to the sun rather than vice versa. Now the sun is the other, the distant object; while the earth is like the human self, or the subject—it is the home of us human subjects, after all, is it not?

KANT: Yes.

SOCRATES: But your revolutionary idea is that in human knowing the object known is relative to the knowing subject rather than vice versa as everyone used to think. Isn't that right?

KANT: Yes. I see why you would think my idea is just the reverse of Copernicus', Socrates. But in another way, it is not. Think of the motion of the sun and the stars across the horizon from their rising to their setting. The ancient, naïve, uncritical belief was that this motion was real. But Copernicus denied that assumption and said that this motion is only apparent, not real; that it is caused by us, the observers, that is, by the movement of our earth.

SOCRATES: I see your point now, and I accept the aptness of your Copernican analogy. We should not be arguing about analogies and who has the right to them, after all. That is only a question of labels. We should get to the substantive point.

KANT: Again, you exhort us to do so instead of doing so, Socrates.

SOCRATES: Then let us do so.

KANT: May I remind you that you are still exhorting instead of doing?

SOCRATES: You may.

KANT: So when do we do it?

SOCRATES: Now. So your substantive point is that when we think rationally it is we who actively contribute all the form—all the order and structure and intelligibility, all the *logos*—is that correct?

KANT: Yes. And thus all the universality and all the necessity.

SOCRATES: Rather than receiving and mirroring these forms, all these *logoi*.

KANT: Yes.

SOCRATES: So we are active rather than passive with regard to forms?

KANT: Yes.

SOCRATES: Do you say, then, that we *create* forms rather than discovering them?

KANT: No, we do not simply create forms out of nothing. And we certainly do not create the world that we apply these forms to. Human knowing is a cooperative venture, like human sexuality. Just as both a man and a woman are needed to conceive a child, so both a mind and a world, both form and matter, are needed to conceive a concept. Only the form comes from the mind, not the matter, or content. *That* is supplied by sense experience. We simply apply these forms to our sense experience of the world. Thus concepts and percepts work together. As I said, **"concepts without percepts are empty, percepts without concepts are blind."**

CPR A51, B75

SOCRATES: I see. How interesting that the same word, "conception", refers to the origin of both a concept and a baby.

KANT: And in Aristotle's mistaken genetic science, all the form came from the man, who was the source of all the activity and actuality and determination, while the woman was wholly passive and contributed nothing but formless matter. This biological error was a kind of mirror image of his epistemology, in which the mind was the passive matter and the world contributed all the active form.

SOCRATES: So in your epistemology the roles are reversed, and nature is the passive woman while the mind is the active man?

KANT: Not quite. That is too simplistic, Socrates. In my epistemology both of the two sources of human knowledge actively contribute. The mind actively contributes the form, but "things-in-themselves" actively contribute the matter. That is why we feel things constantly impinging on our senses and our minds. Something out there comes to us actively. There is activity on both sides, as in human sexuality.

SOCRATES: Your anthropology seems better than that of Aristotle. That I will grant you. But I wonder about your epistemology.

KANT: What do you wonder about, exactly, Socrates?

SOCRATES: You say all the form comes from us, not from nature. Is that right?

KANT: Yes. In our mind, these are called "concepts". They are the *conceptus*, the mental baby that is conceived when nature and the mind have intercourse.

SOCRATES: But you say the concepts are not concepts *of* objectively real forms, or universals. Is that correct?

KANT: Yes, that is correct. They are not concepts *of* forms, as if the forms are independently real. The concepts—the forms of perception and the categories of logic and the Ideas of Pure Reason—*are* the forms. They are the "transcendental preconditions" of knowledge. They are the way we always must experience the world. They are universal and necessary.

SOCRATES: So you are subjectivizing Aristotle's forms. You make them subjective.

KANT: Not if by "subjective" you mean "*individual*". The forms are universal and necessary. They will always be the same for everyone. They are "subjective" to rational *consciousness itself.*

SOCRATES: All right, so they are *collective* rather than individual. But they are still subjective, not objective. They are like a dream, although it is a shared dream.

KANT: I would not call them a dream, Socrates. I do not say they are merely *collective*—the way *many* individuals think—but *universal*—the way *all* individuals think. And they are not only *universal* but also *necessary*. They are not just how we happen to think but the ways in which we *must* think. No one can think without them. They are not a choice. They are not arbitrary. There is no alternative.

SOCRATES: I understand. But they are still from us, not from the world.

KANT: That is correct.

SOCRATES: Can we use an analogy for this dependence on us? Can we say that the mind is like a sieve, with holes in it? Imagine sand and dirt and rocks being fed into the sieve at random, without any structure. The sieve filters this material. First of all, it simply does not let through some of the material: the bigger rocks. Second, what it does let through, it filters and structures: it sorts the sand into straight lines as it falls through the holes in the sieve, and it falls in the same pattern as the holes in the sieve.

KANT: It is something like that. The mind does filter and sort the materials that enter it. But that is not a radical enough image. For the mind is still passive in your analogy.

SOCRATES: Then let us try a second analogy. How about this one? When we think of anything, we impose these forms on what we think about, like someone wearing a pair of colored eyeglasses that cannot be removed from one's eyes. They are part of the eye itself. And these glasses have, let us say, blue and red lenses, and they impose the colors blue and red, and perhaps purple as the combination of blue and red, on whatever one sees.

KANT: That works well for the senses, for the two forms of all sense perception are space and time, and they work together to construct the spatio-temporal form of the sensory manifold, as red and blue work together to make purple. But my point is not only about sense knowledge; it is also about abstract ideas.

SOCRATES: Then let us talk about the mind. Let's say that the mind is like a person who classifies every religious idea as orthodox or heretical. He imposes that standard on all ideas. Or let's say it is like a person who classifies every idea as radical, progressive, middle-of-the-road, conservative, or reactionary. Does that analogy work?

KANT: That is a somewhat better image. But it still sounds too passive, like a mental sieve.

SOCRATES: Then let me try one more image. Could we say that according to you, knowing is something like baking cookies? Imagine a large machine fixed to a conveyer belt in a large bakery. There are three parts to the machine. The first part of the machine receives the unformed cookie batter and stamps forms on it: the forms of stars, circles, or gingerbread men. The second part of the machine is an oven that bakes the batter hard. And the third part puts the cookies in packages and wraps them. The machine is the mind. All the unformed matter, like the batter, comes from nature, or the world, or the "things-in-themselves", as you call them, outside the mind. But all the form, all the structure, is imposed by the mind itself upon this matter-batter.

KANT: That is a somewhat better analogy.

SOCRATES: Well, I think we have an understanding of what your "Copernican revolution" essentially means, then, which was the first of our four questions. I am tempted to move immediately to the third question, the *consequences* of this idea, which are truly world-shaking, for it affects absolutely everything, like a bomb exploding, or like the sun rising. (You see, I deliberately used both an unflattering and a flattering image.) But I will resist that temptation and take our questions in order. Let us move to our second question, then: *Why* did you adopt this idea?

KANT: It was my answer to Hume, you see. Both Hume and his Rationalist opponents, in fact all philosophers before me, had assumed *that the task of knowledge was to conform to objects*. That was the hidden premise of both schools of thought, their common assumption that I questioned. The dogmatists claimed that knowledge attained its object, but they did not adequately prove this claim. And the skeptics claimed that knowledge failed to attain that object. But both assumed that it was the *task* of knowledge to mirror the object. Both assumed Aristotle's definition of truth: "to say of what is that it is and of what is not that it is not". This is the assumption I questioned. This is how I avoided Hume's skeptical conclusion.

SOCRATES: *Why* did you question Aristotle's "realist" assumption that true thought conformed to reality?

KANT: Because it led nowhere. For on that assumption, you had to choose between one of the two extremes that philosophy *always* seeks to avoid: dogmatism and skepticism, which I found in Rationalism and Empiricism, respectively. You yourself did exactly what I did, Socrates: you refused both dogmatism and skepticism. And that was why both the establishment dogmatists and the sophistical skeptics misunderstood you and feared you and eventually got you executed. And that is also why you questioned everything: dogmatists do not question because they think they already know the answers, and skeptics do not question because they think no one can ever find the answers. Is this not a good description of your position, Socrates, refusing both dogmatism and skepticism?

SOCRATES: It is indeed—though I did not face the problem you did, the epistemological problem, especially the so-called "critical problem", the demand for a critical justification of human reason. That was a new problem raised by Descartes.

KANT: And Descartes' Rationalism simply assumed, dogmatically, that concepts like "cause", "substance", "self", and "God" were derived from reality, even though they were not derived from sense experience. Hume refuted that assumption.

SOCRATES: So would you say that you were closer to Hume's epistemology than to Descartes'?

KANT: I believed Hume was both importantly right and importantly wrong. He was right in pointing out that these concepts were not derived from sense experience, but he was wrong in concluding that they were therefore merely customs or habits. My "Copernican" hypothesis allowed me to avoid both Descartes and Hume, you see.

SOCRATES: Is that all it is, a *hypothesis*? In the famous passage we just read, from the Preface to the second edition of the *Critique*, you presented your new idea simply as an assumption, a supposition, a possibility, a thought-experiment.

KANT: That is correct.

SOCRATES: So you do not claim to *prove* it?

KANT: "The proof of the pudding is in the eating", as they say. The hypothesis has better results than any other. It alone enables me to escape the dilemma of Rationalism versus Empiricism.

SOCRATES: But surely that last statement of yours is simply not true. Your "Copernican revolution" is not in fact the only way anyone ever avoided that dilemma. Our previous conversation discovered a fourth possibility, a fourth epistemology, which also did precisely that.

KANT: You mean Aristotle's philosophy?

SOCRATES: Yes.

KANT: So you are saying that Aristotle's philosophy and mine are equally possible hypotheses because both fulfill this desired task of avoiding both Rationalism and Empiricism?

SOCRATES: Yes. Or perhaps your philosophy and his are *not* equal. Perhaps his is better.

KANT: Why might that be? I cannot think of any possible reasons for thinking that. Can you?

SOCRATES: I can think of at least three possible reasons, though I do not know how strong these reasons are until we investigate them.

First, Aristotle agrees more than you do with common sense on this question.

KANT: That is only a social or emotional advantage, which is not intrinsic to the issue but extrinsic. It is not a philosophical advantage until it is shown that it is more rational.

SOCRATES: I grant you that.

KANT: What is your second reason?

SOCRATES: That his philosophy also gives us the possibility of a *metaphysics* that is neither dogmatic nor skeptical. For on the one hand it does not dogmatically assume the existence of the Rationalists' innate ideas not derived from experience, which Empiricists like Locke and Hume refuted. Nor, on the other hand, does it limit itself to Empiricism, and thus it avoids the skeptical result that we cannot know any universal forms or principles, and thus no metaphysics.

KANT: So does mine. So Aristotle's philosophy is only equal to mine in that way, but not better.

SOCRATES: But it seems to offer more to metaphysics than yours does because it gives us knowledge that is not just transcendental but transcendent, not just subjective but objective.

KANT: It *claims* to do that. But since it does not address "the critical problem", it does not justify that claim, as mine does.

SOCRATES: Your argument here assumes, of course, that "the critical problem" is a legitimate one.

KANT: What do you mean by a question that is "legitimate"?

SOCRATES: At least this: one that can be answered and one that does not contradict itself.

KANT: And you question both of those assumptions.

SOCRATES: I do.

KANT: Some time I shall have to read the account of your conversation with Descartes, where you develop that argument. Now what is your third reason?

SOCRATES: That perhaps your epistemology does *not* avoid the vices of *either* the Rationalist or the Empiricist, as you claim to do.

KANT: Why not, for goodness' sake?

SOCRATES: Because you too posit innate ideas, in fact *three* sets of innate ideas. And instead of deriving them *from* experience by abstraction, you impose them *on* experience. That sounds more rationalistic than Rationalism.

KANT: They are not ideas, Socrates; they are just empty categories.

SOCRATES: But they are much more than a "blank slate". And they are *innate* categories.

KANT: And how do you say I do not avoid the vices of Empiricism?

SOCRATES: The vice you saw there was skepticism, was it not?

KANT: Yes.

SOCRATES: But you seem to be even more skeptical than Hume.

KANT: Why do you say that, for goodness' sake? My conclusions are very far from his. *I* do not say to burn all the library books whose reasoning is not based on either "relations of ideas" or "matters of fact", as *he* does. In fact, I allow for even a transcendental metaphysics.

SOCRATES: Because Hume at least says that we can know some things as they really are, some "matters of fact", like "the sky is blue". But you deny that we can ever know *any* "things in themselves", but only appearances—the appearances that *we* have structured.

KANT: So, to your mind my philosophy is really a form of skepticism?

SOCRATES: It seems like it. But it also seems to be a form of dogmatism.

KANT: Why? Because of my innate forms? I deduce those; I do not dogmatically assume them.

SOCRATES: Yes, you do—although most philosophers will find this "transcendental deduction of the categories" the most questionable section in all of your *Critique of Pure Reason*. But the main reason I call your philosophy dogmatic is because you treat this

Copernican "hypothesis" of yours as more than a hypothesis. You do not prove it. You do not give any reason for believing this idea of yours except that it avoids the problems of Descartes and Hume. You do not deduce it from any premises.

KANT: But it is a consistent hypothesis.

SOCRATES: We shall explore that shortly.

KANT: Can you give me a preview? Can you summarize briefly the reason you think my "Copernican revolution" is inconsistent?

SOCRATES: I have alluded to that already. If Aristotle is wrong about knowledge mirroring reality and you are right about reality mirroring knowledge, it seems that you still have to assume and use his old notion of truth when you say that your new notion of truth is *true*, or the way things really are.

KANT: That is a serious charge, Socrates.

SOCRATES: I have not yet come forth with the most serious one of all.

KANT: What is that?

SOCRATES: That there is a price for believing in your revolutionary idea. We must give up something precious for it.

KANT: What price? What must we give up?

SOCRATES: We must give up the whole of the task of philosophy as it was so nobly conceived by two thousand years of philosophers before you. We must cease claiming to know truth, at least what ordinary people mean by truth. We cannot do what we most want to do: to know things in themselves.

I will tell you what we are like if your philosophy is true. We are like two castaways on a desert island who find a message in a bottle washed up in the waves. Thinking it is from the outside world, they read it, and to their chagrin they discover that it is only the message they wrote themselves. What a disappointment! But that is the status of all our so-called knowledge if your hypothesis is correct.

KANT: I do not accept the fittingness of your analogy, Socrates. The emotional response of the two castaways is naturally sad. But there is no need for that sad response to my "Copernican revolution".

SOCRATES: There is, if what you want to know is the truth of things, or objective truth, or the truth about objective reality. You say we cannot know "things-in-themselves"; that has to be bad news to philosophers, for that was precisely their quest.

KANT: But perhaps they were wrong in thinking that that was their quest!

And even if not—even if they were right and we must "pay the price", as you put it—still, the price for abandoning that quest is worth paying.

SOCRATES: Why? Because the quest is in vain anyway?

KANT: Yes. And also for a more positive reason: because with my new philosophy I have fulfilled two other crucial quests. I have saved science from Hume's skepticism by restricting it to phenomena, and I have saved both morality and religious faith from his skepticism by placing them beyond the possibility of being refuted by science. As I wrote, **"I have therefore** CPR B **found it necessary to deny** *knowledge* [of things- xxx in-themselves] **to make room for** *faith.*"

SOCRATES: I cannot think of a single one of the great religious founders who would agree with that bargain and that strategy.

KANT: Why not?

SOCRATES: They would all claim that faith gives us a kind of *knowledge* of God, or of spiritual reality, a kind that reason does not give. The consequences for religion of your denial that we can have any knowledge of things-in-themselves would seem to be rather like the consequences of a bomb on a city.

KANT: No. The consequences are good. They *save* the city from the bombs.

SOCRATES: Those bombs: From whom do they come?

KANT: That's exactly right, Socrates, from Hume do they come, and not from me.

SOCRATES: Why, Immanuel, what a dangerous place this is for you! You have already caught a strange infection from your association with me: you have learned how to make bad puns.

KANT: But seriously, what I have learned, and not from you, is how to save religion from the encroachments of science. I have made peace in the great modern war between these two great human enterprises, the war that has been tearing Western civilization apart.

SOCRATES: You have done so only by surrendering both armies, the armies of religion and the armies of science, by denying the fundamental claim of each of them: the claim of science to know the true universe and the claim of religion to know the true God.

KANT: But both claims are impossible to fulfill. For both claims are arrogant and unthinking, Socrates. They are uncritical. Especially the religious one. How could the mind of mere mortal man know the secret things of the Creator?

SOCRATES: You must know the answer to that question yourself, Emmanuel. Any Christian, and any Muslim or religious Jew as well, would know this answer.

KANT: I do indeed know that answer because it is written in my name: "Immanuel" means "God with us". God is so much "with us" that His name is written on our hearts. He is an essential idea of all human consciousness, as I show in my philosophy. Like self and world, God is a necessary Idea of Pure Reason.

SOCRATES: But surely the God of the great religions is not an *Idea* but a real Person.

KANT: Are you suggesting another answer to the question of how man can know his Creator?

SOCRATES: Of course.

KANT: And what other answer is that?

SOCRATES: The one that nearly all Christians, Jews, and Muslims have given for many centuries: divine revelation. It is the idea that since the mind of mere mortal man cannot know the secret things of God, that is precisely why God spoke and revealed to man the things he could not otherwise know but needed to know.

KANT: Oh, I believe that too. But I believe that revelation is embedded in the very structure of nature and of morality. Remember my favorite saying: **"Two things fill the mind with . . . admiration and awe . . . the starry heavens above me and the moral law within me."** Prac 85

SOCRATES: But according to your "Copernican revolution", all that we can know of "the starry sky above" is what we have already structured by our act of knowing it, and *not* these things as they are in themselves. And you will claim in your ethics that all we can know of "the moral law within" is what we have already willed by our own rational will, or practical reason, which you claim is autonomous.

KANT: Yes.

SOCRATES: And now you say that this is how God reveals Himself?

KANT: Yes.

SOCRATES: So divine revelation is identical with human reason and will?

KANT: Exactly! See? I have fulfilled the medieval quest of a synthesis of faith and reason much more completely than any of them ever did.

SOCRATES: I wonder how an *identification* of faith and reason could be a *synthesis* of them. Is that not like saying that a union of two people of the same sex fulfills the task of a synthesis of man and woman better than a heterosexual union does? Must this not be a *reduction* of faith to reason, or of reason to faith, or of both to some third thing that is neither?

KANT: You are arguing by analogy, Socrates.

SOCRATES: That is true.

KANT: And analogies cannot be proofs.

SOCRATES: That is also true. But they can be clues.

KANT: Clues are not proofs, or even arguments, as you well know.

SOCRATES: I know. But my point is simply this: Whether you are right or wrong in your philosophy, it is not what the great religions say. They say that they reveal objective truth, while you say this is impossible for us to know. And therefore it seems to be a great confusion on your part to claim that you are the defender of religion rather than "the Destroyer", as Heine labeled you.

Indeed, there does not seem to be a single one of the ancient Christian teachings that is not stood on its head if it is reinterpreted by your "Copernican revolution", and subjectivized: God, the Creation, the Fall, the Redemption, Providence, miracles, the Incarnation, the Resurrection, the Church, Scripture, the Sacraments, the Commandments—every one of them, if made to attend your school of philosophy, seems to come out standing on its head.

KANT: Perhaps this is their right position. Perhaps all these religions were mistaken in their ancient claims, and perhaps only some such revision as mine can save religion and make it intellectually believable in an age of enlightenment.

SOCRATES: But if so, if you are thus saving religion, you seem to be saving it from itself. You are not saving the claims of any religion in its original form.

Not any Western religion, at any rate. Perhaps Hinduism would survive your "Copernican revolution", since it does not believe in objective truth anyway, since Brahman never creates a real world, but only dreams it. But, then, Hinduism was never threatened by Western science or by David Hume in the first place.

KANT: I cannot agree with your alarming and apocalyptic fear that my philosophy will destroy religion. For one thing, philosophy is not religion and religion is not philosophy and each is independent of the other. If each is independent of the other, then religion is independent of philosophy, so that even if my philosophy is wrong, that will not imperil religion. Religion stands on other foundations than philosophical foundations. It stands on faith. Philosophy stands on reason.

SOCRATES: Even if all this is granted, is it not also true that the philosophies of any age are the seedbed of religion, as reason is the precondition for faith?

KANT: What do you mean?

SOCRATES: Do you remember the Gospel parable of the sower?

KANT: Yes.

SOCRATES: What made the difference between the seed that sprouted and the seed that died?

KANT: How it was received by the soil.

SOCRATES: Exactly. It was not the seed itself, nor the sower, but the prior condition of the soil that made the difference between belief and unbelief, or between a real and lasting belief and one that died. Now if you remember the parable, what is symbolized by the seed?

KANT: The gospel, the religion, the divine revelation. But the reception of that is a matter of faith, not reason.

SOCRATES: True. But what made some seed grow and others not?

KANT: The different soils.

SOCRATES: So the soil is the precondition for faith. Is not the soil then natural reason, or the philosophies put forward by natural reason?

KANT: I suppose that is part of it, yes.

SOCRATES: And the rocky or thorny or shallow ground did not allow the seed to grow. So a rocky or thorny or shallow philosophy might not allow religious faith to grow. In that way, even though your philosophy is a matter of reason and not faith, it may not allow religious faith to grow.

And there surely seems to be such a connection. If your philosophy is accepted, and we believe that we cannot know things-in-themselves, does this not make an immense difference in how we must interpret divine revelation and how we must interpret religious faith in that revelation? Might your philosophy thus not indeed turn religious faith upside down, just as I have said?

KANT: Even if this is so, even if it entails a religious revolution, it is necessary. For my philosophy is the only way to *save* religion from the critiques of it by modern science.

SOCRATES: Have you tried any other way? There are others, you know.

KANT: I have not seen any other way that works. And mine works admirably and simply, at one stroke. For if my "Copernican revolution" is true, then all our science comes from the use of one set of eyeglasses, so to speak, and religion and morality comes from another. So I preserved both science and religion, and ended their warfare, by first restricting and then distinguishing their spheres of jurisdiction. Such a neat and elegant solution! How can you be so negative about it?

SOCRATES: Because in my experience what is true is not neat and elegant but messy and surprising. And should not philosophy also be messy and surprising?

KANT: Only if we accept both of your premises: that reality is messy and that philosophy is supposed to mirror reality.

SOCRATES: And you deny both of those premises, or at least the second one. So we are back where we started.

KANT: I would like to question you for a moment, Socrates, if you don't mind.

SOCRATES: I don't mind. It is my task to raise questions, but sometimes answering questions is a way of raising them.

KANT: Would you please tell me how else you would save religion and science from each other? How else would you meet the threats to both that emerged in my time, especially from Hume?

SOCRATES: Perhaps the threats from which you thought you saved both science and religion were not so serious at all. And perhaps your cure was worse than the disease.

KANT: Oh, no, the threats were very real. The threat of science was not merely the threat *against* science launched by Hume's skepticism, but also the threat *from* science to reduce man and the human element to nothing but a tiny cog in the great cosmic machine. As I said once to an astronomer who argued that "astronomically speaking, man is utterly insignificant", "Sir, you are forgetting that astronomically speaking, man is the astronomer."

SOCRATES: That is a striking saying. But what, exactly, did you mean by it?

KANT: That the man who trembled at the clockwork universe trembled at the phantoms of his own mind. Because of my "Copernican revolution", the message in the bottle is indeed from ourselves, as your picture of the castaways puts it. But this is good news rather than bad. We meet ourselves, not a stranger, in meeting the universe. It is the universe that we ourselves have structured, as an artist structures his painting.

SOCRATES: But where is the wonder then? Where is the wonder of the artist at natural beauty? And where is the wonder of the nonartist at the art? We do not wonder at ourselves, unless we are great egotists.

KANT: But I was very sensitive to wonder. One more time I must ask you to remember my favorite saying: **"Two things fill the mind with . . . admiration and awe . . . the starry heavens above me and the moral law within me."** Prac 85

SOCRATES: Then you must be a great egotist indeed, if you really believe that these things are "only from ourselves", like the message in the bottle.

KANT: To use your analogy, I saved all three messages —of science, of morality, and of religion—from the threat of being lost at sea by putting them into the bottle of Reason.

SOCRATES: But all three wanted to be free from the bottle.

KANT: What do you mean by that?

SOCRATES: They all want to get out of the bottle and into the world. Surely the scientist wants to know what the universe really is, not only how we make it to appear by projecting our forms and categories upon it. And surely the moralist wants to know what is *really* good and evil, not only what we make to be good and evil by our reason and will legislating the law, as you say we do in morality. And surely the person of religious faith wants to put that faith in the *real* God, the true God, not in any human construction, however universal and necessary it may be.

KANT: I thought *you* would be more sympathetic to my restriction of knowledge, Socrates. You were always on the verge of skepticism.

SOCRATES: When I met dogmatists, yes. But not when I met skeptics, like the Sophists.

KANT: Do you suspect I am a Sophist?

SOCRATES: No, but I suspect you are too close to them. I suspect you are unduly under the spell of Hume.

KANT: But I cannot simply ignore his critique. And how else can I answer it?

SOCRATES: I had a conversation with him here a short time ago. You might get some ideas from that.

6

Is Kant's "Copernican Revolution" Self-Contradictory?

SOCRATES: I would like to focus our conversation for a while on the most serious criticism of your most serious idea: the charge that your "Copernican revolution" is logically self-contradictory.

KANT: And why do you say it is logically self-contradictory?

SOCRATES: Oh, I do not *say* that it is. I *ask* whether it is. And I ask *you*. We are not here to debate my philosophy versus yours—I do not even claim to have one —but only to explore yours. I am not your enemy, like a soldier in a war, but your friend, like a doctor. I am your diagnostician, so to speak.

KANT: And you seem to see something like a disease in my philosophy?

SOCRATES: If we can call self-contradiction a philosophical disease, yes.

KANT: Where do you see this disease?

SOCRATES: Right at the heart of your central idea, your "Copernican revolution".

KANT: Can you show me this disease?

SOCRATES: I think so, if you will only follow me slowly and carefully, step by step.

KANT: That is what good philosophers do, after all.

SOCRATES: Well, then, let us begin with something that is not only not self-contradictory, but is self-evident: that you are aware of something.

KANT: You want to start where Descartes started, with "I think, therefore I am"?

SOCRATES: No. Descartes ignored the question of what he thought about and concentrated only on the fact that he was thinking. I do not want to make that questionable move. I only want you to admit that you are thinking about something, or conscious of something, or aware of something, or cognizing something.

KANT: That seems to be an innocuous starting point.

SOCRATES: Oh, I think it is more than innocuous. I think it is self-evident. In other words, it is self-contradictory to deny it.

KANT: Why?

SOCRATES: Well, what would be the logical contradictory of "I am aware of something"?

KANT: "I am *not* aware of something."

SOCRATES: Yes. And that means "I am not aware of anything"; "I am not aware of anything at all." Isn't that what it means?

KANT: Yes.

SOCRATES: And do you see why that is self-contra-dictory?

KANT: Of course. If I am not aware of anything at all, I cannot think that or say that, because thinking or saying *that* is being aware of *that*, and thus being aware of *something*.

SOCRATES: Exactly.

KANT: Where are you going with this, Socrates? What does this have to do with my "Copernican rev-olution"?

SOCRATES: Be patient, please. You will soon see. Here is my second point. See whether or not you follow me here. If you are aware *of something*, does that not nec-essarily imply that you are aware of something that is somehow different than your mere act of awareness itself?

KANT: Yes, I believe it does. That is the meaning of "awareness"; that is its own essential and intrinsic structure. So you are not beginning with Descartes' bare "cogito".

SOCRATES: No. I am beginning with what seems to be common to all human cognitive experience. All thinking is a thinking *of something*, and the object of thought is something other or more than the sub-jective act of thinking about it.

KANT: Yes, but that "something" need not be a "thing-in-itself". Are you presupposing that it is? If so, you are *presupposing* that my "Copernican revolution" is not true rather than proving it.

SOCRATES: Not at all. My point here, about the object of thought being *different* from the act of thinking, is true whether you are right or wrong about the object of thought being *formed* by the act of thinking it. For whatever the object of thought is, and whatever its relation to our awareness of it may be— whether it is constructed by our awareness of it, as you say, or whether it is independent of our awareness, as thinkers before you said—in either case it is the *object* of thought, not the *subject* of thought or the *act* of thinking.

KANT: Yes. But again I must protest. I suspect you are presupposing that my "Copernican" epistemology is wrong from the beginning of your argument rather than proving it at the end.

SOCRATES: Why do you say that?

KANT: Because the act of thinking and its object are always relative to each other. Do you deny that? If so, I think you are again begging the question and presupposing the "pre-Copernican" theory of knowledge that you are trying to prove against me. For you are presupposing the independence of the object of thought from the act of thinking.

SOCRATES: I do not deny that the act and its object are always relative to each other. In fact, I affirm it. For whether or not the real *"thing-in-itself"* is independent of the act of thinking, the *object-of-thought* is not. For when anything becomes an object-of-thought, it becomes an object-*of-thought* and thus enters into that relationship to thought. "Thing" and "object" do not mean the same thing. "Object" adds something to "thing". It adds exactly what you say: a relationship to thought.

But I think this admission, this correlativity between the knowing subject and the known object, does not cast any doubt at all upon my point that the object of thinking is somehow *other* than the subject. Just follow my argument here. . . .

KANT: I will try.

SOCRATES: A and B can be *relative* to each other only if A and B are in some way *other* than each other, isn't that so? For if A is simply A, and in no way other than A, then we do not say that A and A are "relative" to each "other", do we?

KANT: No.

SOCRATES: So then there is a subject of thinking, or a thinker; and there is an object of thinking, or a something-thought-about.

KANT: I admit that. But I say not only that the object-of-thought is *relative to* the thinking subject or the act of thinking, but also that the object-of-thought is *not independent of* the thinking subject or of the act of thinking. I say that its form (though not its existence) is *dependent* on the thinker and the act. That is my contention. That is my "Copernican revolution".

SOCRATES: I think I may be able to disprove your contention by using the premise you yourself just admitted.

KANT: You think you can prove your conclusion that the object is *independent* of the subject by arguing from our agreed premise that the object is *other* than the subject?

SOCRATES: Yes.

KANT: No. You cannot do that. They are two distinct propositions, and the one does not logically follow from the other.

SOCRATES: I think it does.

KANT: How?

SOCRATES: Do you say that the object is dependent on the mind, and that it is constructed by the mind's act of knowing?

KANT: I say that its knowable forms and structures are, yes. Not its very existence. It is "constructed" not in the sense of being "created" out of nothing, but in the sense of being "formed".

SOCRATES: I understand. So if it is formed, it is formed out of something.

KANT: Indeed.

SOCRATES: Out of something that is unformed before it is formed.

KANT: Of course. That is true by definition.

SOCRATES: Out of something that was first unformed, and then it is formed.

KANT: Yes.

SOCRATES: It is formed when our thinking thinks it.

KANT: That is correct.

SOCRATES: And this unformed matter is the raw material given in sensation.

KANT: That is true *for reason*. Reason imposes categories on sensation. But even within sensation there is a prior forming. We form our sensations by imposing what I call the two "forms of sensibility"— time and space. That is why everything that we can ever sense or imagine is limited to the temporal and spatial.

SOCRATES: I understand. So you say that the object we know, the object of our cognition, is *not* the thing-in-itself, the "noumenon", but only the appearance, the "phenomenon".

KANT: Yes, that is what I say: that all human cognition is limited to phenomena.

SOCRATES: Let's use "A" for the "thing-in-itself" and let's use "AB" for the phenomenon that is formed by our imposing our forms and structures on A.

KANT: Why not just say "noumenon" and "phenomenon" or "thing-in-itself" and "object-of-knowledge"?

SOCRATES: You will see in a moment. My justification for the letters right now is this: You say that AB is a composite thing, do you not? That its matter, and its existence, come from outside us, but its form and intelligibility come from inside us. Isn't that correct?

KANT: Correct. So we never know A apart from AB.

SOCRATES: I see a logical problem here.

KANT: What is it?

SOCRATES: A is not known, but formed by our act of thinking, correct?

KANT: Correct.

SOCRATES: Is AB also formed and constructed by our act of thinking it, as A is?

KANT: Hmm. . . . What if I say no?

SOCRATES: Then we know it as a thing-in-itself.

KANT: We do *not* know it as a thing-in-itself.

SOCRATES: Then your answer must be yes. AB is also formed by our act of thinking it.

KANT: Yes.

SOCRATES: Then we seem to have infinite regress. For in that case, just as we did not know A but only AB, because we cannot know any thing-in-itself independent of our thinking, then for the very same reason, we do not know AB either, but only ABC, which is not AB in itself but only AB *as we think it*, C being the act of forming AB into AB-as-thought, which is ABC. Or, if you prefer, C is the forms themselves with which we form AB into ABC.

And if we do not know *any* thing in itself, then we do not really know ABC either as it is in itself, but only ABCD, which is ABC *as we think it*. This infinite regress never stops. It is true of everything, no matter how many more steps we add. So we really know nothing but our own endless process of forming the object into something else.

KANT: That is a very simple argument to answer, Socrates. There is no infinite regress because this process of forming the object by knowing it occurs only once. And after it occurs, we have the formed object, the knowable object.

SOCRATES: I see. And then *that* object, the phenomenon as distinct from the noumenon, or AB as distinct from A, is simply known.

KANT: Yes.

SOCRATES: Known as it is in itself?

KANT: Known as what it is, namely, phenomenon. And this stops the series of formings. We do not form again what is already formed. There is no ABC, just AB.

SOCRATES: But if that is so, then you seem to be conceding the pre-Copernican point of the object's independence of the forming subject *when we know AB*.

KANT: No, for AB is already formed and constructed by the mind.

SOCRATES: Yes, but by the *previous*, or *assumed* unconscious acts of the mind on A to construct AB. Not by the new, conscious act of the mind thinking AB.

KANT: Oh. Hmm. . . . I will have to think about that problem

SOCRATES: Indeed. And when you do, will you be apprehending it as it really is, or constructing or reconstructing it?

KANT: I . . .

SOCRATES: It was a clumsy attempt at a joke. I apologize for the clumsiness, but not for the argument.

But I would like to leave this argument now and proceed to another, second form of the charge of self-contradiction, which is even simpler. It is that your "Copernican revolution" is *immediately and directly* self-contradictory. For if we cannot know anything at all about things-in-themselves, then how do we know they even exist? To posit their existence seems self-contradictory: it seems that you are knowing the unknowable, effing the ineffable.

KANT: According to this charge of self-contradiction that you are bringing against me, it is self-contradictory for me to claim to know the *existence* of things-in-themselves without knowing their *nature*, is that it?

SOCRATES: That is the charge, yes. But I do not bring the charge myself; I only bring it from others to see how you will answer it.

KANT: And does the charge say that this is true only of things-in-themselves, or of anything? Is it always self-contradictory to claim to know the existence of anything if you claim that you do not know its nature?

SOCRATES: I think the charge is that that is *always* self-contradictory, and that is why it is also self-contradictory with reference to things-in-themselves.

KANT: The assumption is that it is self-contradictory, therefore, to claim to know the existence of anything if you do not know its nature.

SOCRATES: Yes.

KANT: Then from that same assumption, one must conclude that we cannot say this of God either.

SOCRATES: That logically follows.

KANT: But traditional Christian theology (for instance, Thomas Aquinas) holds exactly that about God: that we can know His existence but not His essence. And it seems quite reasonable to say that about God. So why is it not also reasonable for me to say the same about my "things-in-themselves"?

SOCRATES: That is a good argument. Perhaps it can be answered, perhaps not. But for now let us simply assume that you have successfully answered this second self-contradiction argument and move on to a third one.

Your epistemology tries to limit human knowing, as Hume's did, but in a different way. Is that not correct?

KANT: It is.

SOCRATES: But as a philosopher named Wittgenstein will argue, "to limit thought you must think both sides of the limit."

KANT: Yes.

SOCRATES: But that seems self-contradictory.

KANT: Why?

SOCRATES: Let's look at a different case, for the sake of seeing the point by contrast. Let's look at limiting anything other than thought. Let's look at limiting the physical boundaries of a country.

KANT: Do you mean drawing the limit in thought or actually constructing a new country's boundaries in reality?

SOCRATES: The argument will work either way, for drawing boundaries in mere thought and drawing boundaries in the physical world both involve drawing boundaries in thought, and that is all that must be granted.

KANT: What is the argument, once this is granted?

SOCRATES: To limit a country's boundaries it is not necessary to live outside the country, but it *is* necessary to *think* outside it. And that is no contradiction. But to limit the boundaries of the country of thought, you must *think* outside the boundaries of the thinkable.

KANT: I see the objection.

SOCRATES: Do you also see a way out of it?

KANT: I think so. I think I answer this objection with a distinction: the distinction between *understanding*, which we cannot do for things-in-themselves, and *positing* or *postulating*, which we can do and which our experience gives us good reason to do.

SOCRATES: Perhaps this reply will stand up too if we investigate it more carefully, perhaps not. But rather than taking the time to do that now, let us look at a fourth objection, which also comes under the heading of a self-contradiction argument. And this is the simplest way of all to state the point that your "Copernican" claim seems to contradict itself.

KANT: What *is* the "simplest way to say it"?

SOCRATES: You say that it is impossible to know objective matters of fact, of things-in-themselves, or real situations. But is *that* a knowledge of a matter of fact, of a thing-in-itself, of a real situation?

KANT: Suppose I say no?

SOCRATES: Then it is not *true*, it is not what-is; your philosophy is not the way things are. Your view of the way knowledge works is not *the way knowledge really works*.

KANT: And suppose I say yes?

KANT: Then your philosophy *is* a knowledge of how knowledge really works. And then it is a knowledge of a matter of fact. And then we are back in the contradiction we saw before: knowing as a matter of fact that no one can know matters of fact.

So if your philosophy is really true, then we cannot *know* that it is really true. And if we cannot know what is really true, then we cannot know that *your philosophy* is really true.

KANT: Your objection presupposes the old Aristotelian notion of truth. That is precisely the point my philosophy questions. Surely it is unfair to try to refute a man's philosophy by presupposing the truth of his opponent's philosophy.

SOCRATES: But what do you mean by the "truth" of a philosophy, then?

KANT: I will tell you. . . .

SOCRATES: But *however* you answer that question, you must claim that your answer is "true" or else you are not arguing at all.

KANT: True.

SOCRATES: And thus you fall back on the old notion of truth in the very act of claiming that your new notion of truth is true.

KANT: No, I need not do that and I will not do that.

SOCRATES: Then, if you keep to your new notion of truth consistently—the notion that truth is constructed rather than discovered and mirrored—then you must say that you also "construct" the truth *of your new notion of truth*, as you construct *all* truths; and then we are back in our ABCD infinite regress.

KANT: That is simply the old refutation of skepticism as the self-contradictory claim to know that we cannot claim to know anything.

SOCRATES: It is indeed! For your philosophy seems to be a new and subtler form of skepticism, and all forms of skepticism seem self-contradictory; twist as you will: I know that I do not know; it is true that there is no truth; I am certain that I am not certain; it is an absolute that there are no absolutes; I dogmatically assure you that we cannot be dogmatic; it is a universal truth that there are no universal truths; it is an objective truth that we cannot know objective truth; et cetera, et cetera.

KANT: Those are merely clever sophisms. The details of my system will explain why this is not a contradiction. Do you have any positive, specific substantive critique, rather than merely charges of formal logical self-contradiction?

SOCRATES: There is at least one, I think, and we need to have another conversation about that.

7

The Sexual Analogy for Knowledge and the Ambiguity of "Phenomena"

SOCRATES: You deny that knowing is receiving form, do you not? You say it is actively imposing form, determining the object.

KANT: That is correct. Knowing is active, not passive. Do you deny that?

SOCRATES: No, that seems obviously true by immediate experience. But I wonder whether knowing is not also receptive. You deny that it is, don't you?

KANT: Indeed I do. Knowing cannot be both active and passive with respect to the same form. Activity and passivity are contraries. They are mutually exclusive.

SOCRATES: Yes, but perhaps activity and receptivity are not. You see, one can question your assumption that receptivity is always passivity. Perhaps you confuse these two things.

KANT: I don't understand what you are getting at.

SOCRATES: It is a confusion that seems very easy to make. Let me try to show you. What is the word that literally means "teachable"? It comes from the Latin word *doceo*, "to teach".

KANT: The word is "docile".

SOCRATES: Yes. And when we hear that word what do we tend to think of?

KANT: We tend to think of sheeplike passivity.

SOCRATES: Exactly. But when we think of education, we do not think of a good learner as passive, do we?

KANT: Indeed not.

SOCRATES: Rather, a mind that is teachable must be active in order to be receptive to teaching, receptive to truth. It is like a woman in sexual intercourse.

KANT: Are you saying that minds are like women?

SOCRATES: I see your shock. Perhaps that shock is natural for you. For you have not had much experience or success in understanding women during your life.

KANT: Shouldn't you be explaining your philosophical point instead of psychoanalyzing me?

SOCRATES: I should indeed. So I will try.

A woman is receptive of a man's seed in sexual intercourse, is she not?

KANT: Of course.

SOCRATES: Does that mean she is passive?

KANT: It would seem so, at least physically.

SOCRATES: Not at all! Neither physically nor emotionally. It is an activity to receive a man's seed, or a man's courtship, just as it is an activity for a catcher to receive a baseball from a pitcher, and just as it is an activity for a student to receive knowledge or understanding from a teacher.

KANT: And what is the point of this analogy?

SOCRATES: That it is also an activity for us to receive form and *logos* from the world.

KANT: I see. So your argument is . . . what?

SOCRATES: That the fact that knowledge is active does not logically entail the conclusion that it is not also receptive of form, and thus it does not necessitate your "Copernican revolution".

KANT: But even if that is true, it only shows that pre-"Copernican" epistemology is consistent. It does not show that it is true.

SOCRATES: But if your "Copernican" alternative is *in*consistent, as yours proved to be if our previous conversation was correct, while the pre-"Copernican" one is consistent . . .

KANT: I would say exactly the opposite, Socrates. For your so-called realist epistemology is *not* consistent, and mine is. For yours leads to logical antinomies, and mine does not.

SOCRATES: I think this issue of your famous "antinomies" will require another whole conversation. But before that, I have one more question, which is related to the status of phenomena in your epistemology.

   This too—the status of phenomena—seems to be best understood by a sexual analogy. For phenomena seem to be like the children in knowing, children of the union of the two parents of the mind and the world. Is that right?

KANT: Yes but the father is the mind and the mother is the world. Aristotle said it was the opposite: that the father was the world and the mother was the mind.

SOCRATES: You distinguish "noumena" and "phenomena", things-in-themselves and appearances, isn't that right?

KANT: Yes.

SOCRATES: And you say we cannot know phenomena but not noumena?

KANT: Yes.

SOCRATES: And "phenomena" means "appearances"?

KANT: Yes.

SOCRATES: I find an ambiguity in the term "appearances" or "phenomena" when I read your *Critique*.

KANT: Where?

SOCRATES: I will not go into great detail in your text, but in some passages you seem to imply that "appearances" are appearances *of* something—of the things-in-themselves, which are hidden from us.

KANT: That's right.

SOCRATES: But in other places you seem to imply that appearances are *independent entities*, and you call them "appearances" not because they are relative to the real things behind them but because they are relative to our own knowing processes and structures: as if they are our sole objects of knowledge.

KANT: They are that. They are all that we observe and discover in the world.

SOCRATES: Well, then this seems to be the same ambiguity I find in your predecessors.

KANT: Which predecessors?

SOCRATES: Both the Rationalists like Descartes and Spinoza and Leibniz and the Empiricists like Locke, Berkeley, and Hume.

KANT: What is the ambiguity?

SOCRATES: They all use the term "idea" to mean two things. On the one hand, it is both something intentional and relative to its object, an idea *of* something. On the other hand, it is something itself, the object we know. For instance, Locke begins his "Treatise" with the definition "Idea = object of knowledge."

KANT: What is the problem? We know ideas, and ideas are ideas of things.

SOCRATES: But surely we do not know ideas! Surely we know *by means of* ideas. What we know is reality, real objects. If not, if we know only ideas and not real things, we do not have *knowledge* but only *opinion*, "only ideas".

KANT: I think I can resolve this so-called ambiguity for you, if you wish, Socrates. But it will require some very subtle and technical thinking. . . .

SOCRATES: I do not wish to undertake such a task now. Perhaps some who read this conversation will want to do so on their own, but most will not. For though the ambiguity may seem alarming and large to philosophers, it will probably seem small and innocuous to most readers.

KANT: I see you have more mercy on them than on me.

8

The "Antinomies of Pure Reason"

KANT: Are you finally finished exploring my one central idea, "Copernican revolution in philosophy"?

SOCRATES: I think not. For I have not yet explored what is probably the single most persuasive argument in its favor. At least it is the argument that has convinced most of those who have been convinced and converted by your philosophy.

KANT: I do not know how my philosophy was received in the generations after my death, so you must tell me: What was this argument that the world finally found so persuasive?

SOCRATES: I did not say that the whole world found it persuasive.

KANT: So the world did *not* find even this "most persuasive" argument persuasive?

SOCRATES: You divided the world, Immanuel, almost as your namesake did, into those who did and those who did not believe your radical claim.

KANT: Do you speak of the world of philosophers or the world of ordinary people?

SOCRATES: Both. For philosophy always filters down to ordinary people, and ordinary people's opinions always filter up into the minds of philosophers. There is always influence both ways.

KANT: So what was the argument?

SOCRATES: That traditional metaphysics leads to what you called "the antinomies of pure reason".

KANT: Ah, yes. I am not surprised by that, for I think they constitute a very clear case against transcendent as distinct from transcendental metaphysics. May I summarize my argument?

SOCRATES: Please do. First of all, what do you mean by an "antinomy"?

KANT: I mean by an "antinomy" a logical contradiction that results from a false premise.

SOCRATES: *Any* false result of a false premise?

KANT: No. An antimony is not a single false conclusion that logically results form a false premise, like "Pigs fly, and I am a pig, therefore I fly." That is simple and easy to see, because the way a single false conclusion follows from the false premise is simply by the rules of deductive reasoning.

SOCRATES: How is an "antinomy" different from that?

KANT: First of all, an antinomy is a set of *two* propositions that contradict each other, *both* of which logically result from a false premise.

Second, they follow not merely by immediate deduction according to the rules of formal logic, but in a subtler way.

Third, the premise here is hidden, not overt. It is assumed, not expressed.

SOCRATES: Could you give me an example other than those in your book, so that we can know the *kind* of thing you speak of in your book—the genus—before we look at your specific examples of this kind of genus?

KANT: Yes. In classical Christian theology, there seems to be the antinomy of predestination and free will. It is the antinomy of (a) God's infallible foreknowledge that I will do A rather than B tomorrow and (b) my free will to choose to do either A or B.

These two ideas certainly seem to contradict each other. For if God knows with infallibility and certainty that I will do A tomorrow, then I *cannot* possibly do B tomorrow. But if I *can* do B, if I really have the power to do B, then A is not infallibly predestined.

These two ideas certainly seem to contradict each other, but that is only because both implicitly presuppose something false: that God's knowledge, like ours, is in time; that He peers ahead into the future, like a fortune teller peering into a crystal ball. If the fortune teller is infallible and tells me I will commit a crime tomorrow, I am not free to choose not to commit the crime. And if I *am* free to choose to commit the crime *or not*, then the fortune teller's foreknowledge cannot be infallible.

It is the hidden assumption that God is like a fortune teller that causes the problem of this antinomy. The problem is that both halves of the antinomy seem true, yet they contradict each other, and two contradictory propositions cannot both be true. And the solution is that if we deny the hidden assumption, we no longer have the antinomy. If we remove God's knowledge from time and make Him the eternally present watcher of all events, contemporary to them rather than foreordaining and infallibly predicting them, then we can avoid the antinomy. For while the infallible fortune teller of a future choice makes free will impossible, a present watcher of a free choice does not, even if he is an infallibly correct watcher.

SOCRATES: Thank you for the example. I think anyone can see from this example both the logical structure of an antinomy and the way to solve it: to root out the hidden false assumption.

KANT: Exactly. Now may I explain first my antinomies, then the false assumption behind them?

SOCRATES: Please do.

KANT: When we think about the universe as a whole, when we think about universal principles that must hold true of the universe as a whole, there are four questions that naturally spring to mind:

1. The first question has two parts: one about time and the other about space. Does the universe have a beginning in time, or is it beginningless and eternal? And is the universe unlimited or limited in space, or size?

2. Is there a simplest element, an atom that cannot be divided into smaller parts? Or is everything composed of parts?

3. Are some events in the universe caused by free choice? Or is everything caused by natural necessity?

4. Is there a necessary being? Or is everything contingent in its being? In other words, is there anything that *must* exist, or is everything able to not exist?

SOCRATES: Those are fascinating questions indeed, and nearly all the great philosophers have sought to answer them in one way or the other.

KANT: And both sides have offered equally sound and irrefutable arguments.

SOCRATES: Can you give me an example?

KANT: Yes. Take the time part of the first antinomy. The world can be proved to have a beginning in time, because, if not, then an infinite series of events must already have happened, and a completed infinite series is impossible. But it can also be proved that the world has no beginning in time, for if it did have a beginning, there must have been some reason why it began just then, when it did. But there can be no such reason, for time itself has no particular character and cannot of itself determine when one particular event within it happens at one particular time. As I put it, "time has no causal capability", no ability to bring anything into being.

SOCRATES: Those do both seem to be equally strong arguments.

KANT: And that is why philosophy has not progressed as science has. It has never resolved such questions as these.

SOCRATES: And you say you have unearthed the hidden reason why this is so?

KANT: Yes. It is really very simple: because neither of the two metaphysical hypotheses can ever be refuted by experience, as a scientific hypothesis can.

SOCRATES: That seems to be true. And why, in turn, is *that* so? Do you claim to go deeper and find the cause of that too?

KANT: That is precisely my claim. It is because both sides are presupposing the same false premise: that we can do traditional "transcendent" metaphysics that goes beyond experience and yet tells us meaningful truths.

SOCRATES: So that is how you answer all the antinomies.

KANT: Yes. The antinomies only seem to be real contradictions. They are not. But we can see this only if we find and reject their common false assumption.

SOCRATES: And you say that false assumption is that we can know things-in-themselves?

KANT: Yes. That is the assumption I question by my "Copernican revolution in philosophy".

You see, Socrates, traditional metaphysics claimed we could know certain laws and principles of all reality, some absolutely universal truths—such as: "Every change requires a cause", or "Every thing that is, is good for something", or "The universe is both one ('uni') and many ('versa')." And when philosophers made that assumption, what was the result? No progress. No agreement. Endless arguments without resolution. We still had the same determinists and free-willers, the same theists and atheists, the same

monists and pluralists, the same materialists and spiritualists in my day as we had in your day, Socrates.
Nobody was ever refuted in traditional metaphysics.
Metaphysical propositions were irrefutable because
no experience could ever refute them.

SOCRATES: I see. Twentieth-century philosophers will
call that the falsification criterion of meaningfulness:
if a proposition is not falsifiable in any way, not falsifiable in principle, it is meaningless.

KANT: And showing a self-contradiction is one way
to refute a proposition, or to prove its opposite. And
that is how we falsify what Hume called "relations
of ideas", known by pure reason: what I call analytic
a priori propositions. We find logical contradictions
within the idea. The only *other* way to verify or falsify
a proposition that Hume recognized was sense experience. And that is how we verify or falsify synthetic
a posteriori propositions. But metaphysical propositions are neither analytic, and thus refutable by sheer
formal logic, nor a posteriori, and thus refutable by
sense experience. There is no empirical, physical test
for metaphysical propositions. Metaphysicians could
only speculate, and construct systems of ideas in the
air, and as long as none of those ideas in the system
contradicted any of the other ideas in the system, no
one could refute them. As I put it in an image,

The light dove, cleaving the air in her free   CPR
flight, and feeling its resistance, might imag-   A5
ine that its flight would be still easier in   B9
empty space. It was thus that Plato left the
world of the senses, as setting too narrow

limits to the understanding, and ventured out beyond it on the wings of the ideas, in the empty space of the pure understanding. He did not observe that with all his efforts he made no advance, meeting no resistance that might, as it were, serve as a support on which he could take a stand.

You see, Socrates, a dove cannot fly even better in empty space. It could not fly there at all, because it can fly and make progress only if it meets some resistance from the air. But the Rationalist metaphysician does not base his metaphysics on experience, so he meets no resistance from experience, so he cannot either verify or falsify his metaphysical propositions by experience.

You will not admit my point, though, because you were a Platonist, were you not? Plato got his famous Theory of Ideas, or Theory of Forms, from you, did he not?

SOCRATES: He did not. All I searched for were true definitions, not metaphysical entities.

KANT: Oh. What do you think of what Plato did as your disciple, then? Did he betray you in metaphysics as well as in politics?

SOCRATES: I will not answer that question now, for it is a distraction from our purpose at hand. I will tell you, however, that I have cross-examined Plato here and I have *not* been wholly satisfied with either his metaphysics or his politics, though I have found some very profound truths in both.

KANT: But do you see my point about metaphysical propositions?

SOCRATES: I do see your point, and also your analogy of the dove. In fact, I know of a similar analogy from my own culture. There was a rumor in old Athens that Icarus was a failed chariot driver who was constantly bumping into things when he drove his chariot. He kept bumping into either curbstones or other chariots. So he decided to give up charioteering and build wings and try to fly to the sun because there are no curbstones or chariots in the air.

KANT: I see. Curbstones and chariots here symbolize falsification.

SOCRATES: Yes. Now how do *you* say propositions can be falsified?

KANT: First of all, in general, it must be in the same way they can be verified.

SOCRATES: That seems logical. And how many ways are there?

KANT: I say there are *three* such ways, and my third way makes room for verifying metaphysical propositions, which are synthetic and a priori, but only if the metaphysics is transcendental rather than transcendent. Hume thought there were only *two* ways to verify propositions, and only two kinds of propositions, and that is why he rejected all metaphysics whatever.

SOCRATES: I see. Well, I admit you have an attractive answer to Hume there. You at least remarry the two divorced partners in knowledge, reason and the senses. And you take a middle position between Rationalism and Empiricism.

But the same could be said of Plato.

KANT: I do not see that at all. Plato was a Rationalist.

SOCRATES: Not as much as Parmenides was. Plato "saved the appearances" as Parmenides did not. In fact, Plato's Theory of Forms was his way of escaping the dilemma of Parmenides versus Heraclitus— a dilemma quite similar, in general, to your dilemma of Descartes versus Hume.

KANT: But that dilemma was in metaphysics and mine was in epistemology.

SOCRATES: Both dilemmas were in both fields. Plato's was first of all in metaphysics, but it was also in epistemology. And yours was first of all in epistemology but also in metaphysics.

But historical understanding and sympathy for a philosopher's dilemma must not trump a logical analysis of whether his solution is *true*, whether that philosopher is Plato or yourself. You would certainly agree with that principle, would you not?

KANT: Yes, of course. Why do you ask?

SOCRATES: Because your most influential successor, a man named Hegel, who claimed to be in many ways your disciple, will *not* agree with that. For him, truth itself is historical, and historically relative, and evolves through history.

KANT: That is absurd. This man may be my successor but he is certainly not my disciple.

SOCRATES: Good. That means we do not have to examine *his* thought, which is notoriously difficult. Well, my mind's jury is still out on deciding your philosophy's guilt or innocence, Immanuel. Let me try to tabulate the positive points of your epistemology as I see them so far.

I see the necessity of your question.

I see the cleverness and intelligence of your answer.

I also see the historical advantages of your solution to your historical problem.

I also see certain timeless truths, certain positive insights into the nature of human consciousness, that you teach us in your epistemology. For one thing, that consciousness has a structure, that it is not simply a "tabula rasa", a blank tablet. Of course, Aristotle knew this too; in fact, he first clearly formulated the difference between what logicians called the three "acts of the mind": conception, judgment, and reasoning. He thought, however, that these were not imposed upon the objects we knew, as in your epistemology, but he thought they reflected and corresponded to aspects of reality: that concepts told us *what* things really were, that judgments told us *whether* they were, and reasoning told us *why* they were.

Still another of your points that seems to be true is that consciousness is active, not passive. This does not mean, however, that it is not receptive. As I pointed out, spiritual receptivity, as distinct from physical receptivity, is active and not passive. So your true points so far do not prove your "Copernican revolution".

And yet another valid point is that you implicitly distinguish human consciousness from divine consciousness, or consciousness as such, by limiting human consciousness, though not as severely as Hume did. We saw a logical problem with this—remember Wittgenstein's saying that to draw a limit to thought you must think both sides of the limit. This would seem to entail the conclusion that human thought cannot be limited; yet it seems obvious that human consciousness is indeed limited. It is at least limited in being perspectival: we can not know everything, but only the things that fit into our perspective, our point of view, and our categories, as we see only those colors that register on our senses.

However, this point does not prove your "Copernican revolution" either, for though human colors and categories are *limited*, it does not necessarily mean they are limited in the way you say they are, by the "Copernican" imposition of the knowing subject.

Still another true insight seems to be your "transcendental" method. The question of the necessary conditions of possibility on the subject side for the experience that we have seems to be a legitimate and fruitful question, and philosophers after you will mine many gems from it, including what they will call "phenomenology". But this too does not entail the "Copernican revolution".

So despite my admiration for all these positive points that I find in your epistemology, I am still unconvinced of your main point. For the logical arguments I gave against your central claim, your "Copernican revolution", at the end of our last conversation, seem to stand strong and unrefuted.

9

God

KANT: Are you ready to examine my ethics now?

SOCRATES: I would first like to examine an idea that links your ethics and your epistemology, for it enters both, but only at the end of both. That is the idea of God.

KANT: Ask away, Socrates.

SOCRATES: You saw yourself as a faithful Christian, did you not?

KANT: Yes. Faithful in thought, at least. None of us lives a life that is perfectly faithful to Christ's high morality, I think.

SOCRATES: I think the first thing that will surprise your readers, then, if they know only that you see yourself as a faithful Christian, is your critique of all arguments for the existence of God. It is a critique that future atheists will make good use of.

KANT: I cannot be held responsible for others' misuse of my ideas. The whole point and purpose of my refutation of the arguments for God was not to replace theism with atheism but reason with faith.

SOCRATES: I understand. But if reason tells us nothing about God, how can we know *what* God to have faith in? Does not all faith presuppose some reason?

KANT: Of course. But faith only presupposes *some* rationally graspable meaning to the object of faith, so that I can distinguish faith in the Creator of the universe from faith in Zeus or Brahman. But faith does *not* presuppose a full and clear comprehension of that object. In fact, if God is infinite, He cannot be defined at all, for all definitions limit the thing defined. And certainly Christian faith does not presuppose that reason can *prove* the existence of its object. In fact, it presupposes exactly the opposite, for if reason *could* prove the existence of its object, then we no longer need to have *faith* in that object's existence, and in fact *cannot* have faith. For what we know to be true by proof we cannot at the same time believe to be true by faith.

SOCRATES: Your analysis seems correct there. The question of whether we have faith in a *person* or not, of course, is not the same as the question of whether we have faith in an *idea*. The first is usually called "trust", while the second is usually called "belief". It is conceivable that we may be able to go beyond belief and prove the existence of God by reason; but it would still be true that we need to trust Him with our lives.

KANT: I accept your clarifications, as you accepted mine.

SOCRATES: Then let us look at your critiques of all the arguments for the existence of God.

KANT: Fine. But please keep in mind the context in which I do this. I do not try to prove God's nonexistence. I believe in God's existence. I try only to demolish the claims of reason to prove either theism or atheism. Both claims go beyond the powers and bounds of reason. Both are examples of the fallacy of pre-Copernican metaphysics.

SOCRATES: What are the arguments for God, then, and how do you refute them?

KANT: There are only three.

SOCRATES: Only three? I know of at least twenty-three.

KANT: But they are of only three kinds, three strategies, so to speak. One is the teleological argument, or the argument from design to a Designer. Aquinas' fifth "way" is an example of this. The second is the cosmological argument, from the existence of the finite, changing, imperfect things we see in the universe to an infinite, unchanging, perfect being that supposedly is the only thing that can possibly adequately explain them. And the third is Anselm's "ontological argument", from the very idea or definition or essence of "God" to His existence.

SOCRATES: Of course you reject all these arguments equally because they all are part of traditional pre-critical, pre-Copernican, "transcendent" metaphysics: they try to transcend phenomena.

KANT: Yes.

SOCRATES: Do you also have three different specific objections against the three different arguments?

KANT: Yes. I first show that the other two both presuppose the ontological argument, and then I refute the ontological argument.

SOCRATES: How do you show that the other two presuppose the ontological argument?

KANT: It's a bit complicated, but essentially it's because only the ontological argument defines "God" at the beginning, and the other arguments can't really prove God if they don't define Him.

SOCRATES: In other words, if they don't define Him, they don't know what they are talking about.

KANT: That's a bit too simple, but that's about it.

SOCRATES: What is wrong with the cosmological argument then?

KANT: The cosmological argument tries to prove the existence of a Necessary Being from the existence of contingent beings. But if we ask: "How can there be a 'necessary being'? What does that mean?" we are asking about the *concept* of God. So the concept of God must be set down before we can meaningfully prove His existence. But that happens only in the ontological argument. Only in that argument does the existence of God *follow from* the concept of God.

SOCRATES: Do you mean "follow" logically, by deduction, or "follow" psychologically, by our minds beginning with the concept of God and only then proceeding to try to prove His existence?

KANT: Both. And the "ontological argument" is the only one that does both.

SOCRATES: Your reasons for reducing all other arguments to the "ontological argument" will seem questionable to most people, I think.

KANT: Perhaps. But not as questionable as the "ontological argument" itself. That argument seems to be full of ambiguities, assumptions, and misunderstandings.

SOCRATES: I should think it would be much easier to refute the "ontological argument" than to show that all other arguments depended on it. For that refutation has been done before, not only by empiricists like Hume but also by metaphysicians like Aquinas. How did you do it?

KANT: By pointing out that **"existence is not a predicate"**.

CPR
A598
B626

The argument deduces God's existence from the premise that "God" means "that than which nothing greater can be conceived", or "the being with all conceivable perfections, all positive predicates".

And therefore, the argument concludes, God must also have the perfection of real, objective existence independent of the human mind, since that is a perfection, and a greater perfection than existence merely in the mind, as an idea.

The mistake with this reasoning is that "God exists" is not like "God is wise" or "God is powerful." "God is", or "God exists", does not have a predicate, as "God is wise" does. Existence is not a predicate because it is not a term, and thus it cannot designate an attribute, or an essence, or a nature. It is not a concept. It is *judged*, not *conceived*.

SOCRATES: That's pretty much what Aquinas said too. Scholastic logicians would say it is known in the second act of the mind (judgment), not in the first act of the mind (conception). That criticism does not seem so very original.

KANT: Another way of putting the objection is this: that the term "God" is used ambiguously when St. Anselm tries to deduce God from the idea of "God".

He begins with the premise that "God" means "that than which nothing greater can be conceived", or "that which possesses all conceivable perfections".

Then he adds the second premise, which I have just refuted, that existence independent of the mind, outside the mind, is a perfection.

So he concludes that God possesses existence just as He possesses every other conceivable perfection.

But quite apart from the falsity of the second premise, there is another fallacy in this argument: what logicians call the fallacy of four terms. The term "God" is really two terms, not one. It changes its meaning. In the premise it is merely the idea or definition of God, and this is indicated by putting quotation marks around it. But in the conclusion the quotation marks have disappeared and we are talking about the real God. To be logically consistent, Anselm should have said only that the *idea* of God included the *idea* of existence. He cannot begin with a real God in the premise without begging the question. And if he begins only with the idea of God, that is all he can end with in the conclusion, unless the term changes its meaning.

SOCRATES: As a deliberate agnostic about God but not about logic, I must accept your critique as logically valid. It is also commonsensical. I do not think anyone who is not a philosopher is ever actually persuaded by the ontological argument, however clever it is, and apparently irrefutable by the philosophical beginner. You were kicking a "straw man" when you focused your attention on refuting that argument.

But the more important point, I think, is how God fits into your philosophy. If traditional "transcendent" metaphysics is impossible, how do you get *God* out of your "transcendental" metaphysics?

KANT: To explain that, I must explain some more details of my "Copernican revolution".

SOCRATES: Be my guest.

KANT: My main point, which we have already explored, is that all the form, structure, intelligibility, and order that we find in our knowledge comes not from the object but from the subject. But we have not yet explored in much detail just *which* kinds of structures, and which structures in particular, our knowing imposes on all its objects.

I say there are three such structures, which are universally and necessarily present in all human experience, and thus they are synthetic a prioris.

First there are the two a priori forms of all sensation, space and time. Space is the form of all possible external sensation, and time is the form of all possible internal sensation. And since our sensation of external bodies, in order to be sensation, must also become an internal sensation in our mind, time is thus the a priori necessary form of *all* sensation. We cannot perceive or even imagine anything not in space and time. And this is simply because those are our two "forms of apperception (perception)", and not because we can know that these things really are in space and time as "things in themselves" that our senses simply mirror.

SOCRATES: May I ask a silly question about this?

KANT: Now it is my turn to say "Be my guest."

SOCRATES: If the space and time we experience are not things-in-themselves, does that mean that I did not really fall asleep after I read the first half of your *Critique of Pure Reason*, but that I only thought I did?

KANT: You could not think any other way, Socrates, than to order events temporally by "before" and "after".

SOCRATES: But does that mean I did not really fall asleep after I read your book, as my common sense told me I did?

KANT: It was not an error in judgment, it was an error about the status of concepts.

SOCRATES: In other words, the answer to my question is yes?

KANT: Yes to what?

SOCRATES: That I did not really fall asleep after I read your book; but that is merely the only way in which I can structure sensory objects: by imposing my before-and-after concept of time on them.

KANT: That *is* the only way you can structure sensory objects.

SOCRATES: So I didn't really fall asleep after I read your book, then?

KANT: That is a very strange way of putting it.

SOCRATES: I think that is what *you* do: putting things very strangely. But *is* that what you say? I still have not received an answer to my question. Did I really not fall asleep after I read your book? Is that what you say?

KANT: Here is what I say about that, Socrates. I say that all intuition is sensory and all sensory intuition is necessarily spatial and temporal, and that that is because of the forms of perception.

SOCRATES: So do you say that I did not really fall asleep . . .

KANT: I say that I cannot say what the world is in itself, only how it appears.

SOCRATES: In other, simpler words, your answer to my question is Yes. I did not really fall asleep after I read your book.

KANT: If I am limited to Yes or No, I must say Yes.

SOCRATES: Thank you, Professor. You have finally given me an answer: I didn't really fall asleep after I read your book. I only thought I did. And I think you have just given half your readers reason to suspect that your philosophy is insane, and thus you have given them a reason *not* to fall asleep while reading your book.

Oh, please do not look so confused and pained, my friend, I was only jesting.

KANT: May we complete this inquisition? May I summarize the rest of my transcendental philosophy?

SOCRATES: As someone said before, be my guest.

KANT: Well, then, in the second place, working from the outside in, come the abstract a priori categories of logical thinking, or as I called them the "forms of understanding". These are something like Aristotle's ten categories, but I have amended them to twelve, and made them categories not of nature but of thought. If we are to rationally understand objects, it must be within categories like substance, causality, relation, and so forth. And this is the way I rescue the categories of substance and causality from Hume's critique of them.

SOCRATES: So these twelve categories too may not be really "there", in the "things-in-themselves".

KANT: We cannot know that they are "there". But they are necessarily "here".

SOCRATES: So perhaps I was really not *really* the cause of my sons. And perhaps I was not *really* related to Xanthippe as her husband. I fear this philosophy of yours will be a bit of a shock to my family.

KANT: This is another jest, I assume?

SOCRATES: Not all your assumptions are questionable, my friend.

KANT: I found the proper home for the categories, especially causality and substance, and I thus answered the arguments of David Hume and overcame skepticism.

SOCRATES: We must investigate this claim of yours also. For there seem to be problems here. For I seem to see a self-contradiction in your answer to Hume.

KANT: Somehow, I am not surprised by that. You find self-contradictions in as many places as medieval monks found devils.

SOCRATES: I know nothing about devils, but I do know something about self-contradictions. And here is the one I seem to see. It will take a while to explain.

Hume's skepticism can be summarized as resting mainly on two premises.

The first premise is that all knowledge of real matters of fact—"matters of fact" as distinct from mere merely logical "relations of ideas"—that dares to go beyond present sensation and memory, rests on the reality of causality, on a real relationship of cause and effect. The example Hume gave was a letter from a friend postmarked in Paris. We believe the friend was in Paris because we reason from the letter, as his effect, to the writer, as its cause.

The second premise is that we do not perceive causality itself, nor are causal relationships self-evident ideas like $2 + 2 = 4$. We cannot deduce the *idea* of an egg from the idea of a bird; we know eggs and birds and the fact that eggs come out of birds, only by sense experience. Hume's conclusion is that we have no knowledge of matters of fact beyond our own sense perception and memory.

Since we did not perceive it, Hume asked where we got the idea of causality. And he answered that it was merely custom, or habit: we see eggs and birds together so often that we associate them and assume birds *"cause"* eggs. Causality is merely psychological, or subjective, according to Hume.

Now your strategy is to make a virtue of necessity, to make a positive point of Hume's negative point. You accept Hume's point that causality is psychological rather than ontological, subjective rather than objective. But you make this part of *reason*. You say that causality is one of the "categories" of reason that we impose on the material world to make it ordered, to unify and interrelate phenomena.

Is that correct?

KANT: This is essentially correct, though vastly oversimplified. Now where do you see a self-contradiction in this answer to Hume?

SOCRATES: You say that causality is a subjective category—"subjective" in the sense of being mental rather than ontological, or, in your terminology, "transcendental rather than transcendent". Is that right?

KANT: Yes. But I hope you understand that that does not mean "subjective" in the sense of being individual and arbitrary rather than universal and necessary.

SOCRATES: I understand that. But though it is universal and necessary, it is only subjective.

KANT: Yes.

SOCRATES: And you say this category is actively imposed by our minds upon all our sense perceptions to create order. Is that right?

KANT: Yes. But I do not say that all the activity comes from the mind. We experience objects as impinging upon our consciousness, so we know there is more than just our consciousness. I am not an Idealist. There is a material world out there. But we cannot know it as it is in itself, only as it is formed by our categories. And one of those categories is causality.

SOCRATES: So you say our knowledge is the result of two things, not just one: the things-in-themselves and our categories such as causality.

KANT: That's right.

SOCRATES: And these two things are something like matter and form for Aristotle, but you say that the form that we experience in all our knowing comes not from the known object but from the knowing subject. Is that right?

KANT: Yes.

SOCRATES: So the order we see or think is caused by two things: objective reality, which we cannot know, transcendently, and our categories, which we can know, transcendentally, as the condition of possibility for our knowledge. Is that right?

KANT: Yes. Where is the self-contradiction in all this?

SOCRATES: Here: If, as you say, causality is only a formal category of our thought, and not an objective reality, how then can our knowledge be *really caused* by these two things—namely, by mere *categories* like "causality" and by the formless and unknowable "things in themselves"?

KANT: Oh. It is a different kind of "causality". Categories do not "cause" knowledge in the same way as birds "cause" eggs.

SOCRATES: I understand that these are two different kinds of causality. Aristotle would call the relationship between bird and egg one of "efficient" causality, and the relationship between categories and the things classified by them "formal" causality, whether the causality is objective, as he thought, or subjective, as you think. But two different kinds of causality are still two different kinds *of causality*. There is something generically the same, and that generic sense —something like real contingency or dependence of the effect on the cause—is the sense in which you seem to contradict yourself.

KANT: My system explains how it works very differently than Aristotle did and in different terminology. You have to read my whole book to understand how it works.

SOCRATES: I don't see how that will help.

KANT: Why not?

SOCRATES: Because to explain the mechanism of a self-contradictory system is not to remove the contradiction.

KANT: In my case, I think it is. Do you want to go into a detailed examination of this point now?

SOCRATES: No, this is another rather technical question whose examination we should rather defer until another time. I am most interested in exploring your third set of formal structures, because this is where God fits in.

KANT: Yes. And self and world. Most interior of all to reason are these three "Ideas of Pure Reason": the ideas of self (or soul), cosmos (or world), and God.

SOCRATES: Could you explain how you derive them or explain them? Where do they come from? Why they are necessary?

KANT: The idea of the world unifies all sensory phenomena: they are all phenomena *in* the single "world". The idea of the self unifies all psychological phenomena: all that is experienced, however diverse, is experienced by one and the same experiencing subject, which I call myself. And the idea of God unifies absolutely.

SOCRATES: I see how you derive the world as the unity of all material objects, but how do you derive the self?

KANT: As the subjective unity of all the perceptions of those diverse objects that constitute the objective unity we call the "world". This unity of the perceiver must transcend the world of objects. For the self that perceives objects is not an object of perception but a subject of perception. It is like the eye that sees objects and brings all visible objects together in one visual field: the eye is not itself a part of that visual field, but transcends it, like a searchlight that illumines things in the sky or the ground but is not itself one of the things it illumines. Similarly, the self that thinks the world into categories, or thinks categories into the world, cannot be itself merely one of the categories or one of the things in the world.

SOCRATES: And where does God come in?

KANT: As the world is transcendent relative to its ingredients and unifies all those ingredients into a single world, and as the perceiving self is transcendent relative to the world perceived and unifies all the acts of perceiving into a single perceiver—so God is absolutely transcendent and unifies both world and perceiving self. He is the ultimate unconditioned condition of all experience.

SOCRATES: I see. So that is why all cultures have some concept, however blurred, of a world, a self, and a God.

KANT: Yes.

SOCRATES: It seems very natural to classify everything into these three classes. For everything must be either less than ourselves, or ourselves, or more than ourselves. Our cosmos is less than what we are, and God is more than what we are. So this is why all cultures have these three ideas.

KANT: That is the way you pre-Copernican metaphysicians spoke, as if you could know these three things as objectively real entities.

SOCRATES: But all cultures do just that.

KANT: I'm not sure they do.

SOCRATES: But if they do, then all cultures are wrong?

KANT: Yes.

SOCRATES: Why are they wrong?

KANT: Why are they right? That's the question. You are assuming uncritically that they are right merely because they are in the majority.

SOCRATES: No, but I am assuming that the onus of proof should be on you as the revolutionary, the upstart, the rebel, especially the rebel against a nearly universal consensus. You do admit that this idea is a "revolution in philosophy".

KANT: Because if you assume what you say they all assumed, you get the antinomies.

First, when you try to think of the world as a thing-in-itself you get antinomies about the world: reason can prove that it is finite in space *and* that it is infinite in space; that it is infinitely divisible *and* that it is not.

And when you try to think of the self as a thing-in-itself, you get the antinomies about the self: reason can prove that the self is free *and* that it is not free but part of the chain of causes in nature.

And when you try to think of God as a thing-in-itself, you get the antinomies about God: reason can prove that a necessary being must exist *and* that it cannot exist.

SOCRATES: Are you saying that perhaps God does not really exist outside the mind, independent of my thought?

KANT: I am saying that we cannot *know* that God exists that way. We cannot prove it or perceive it, we can only *believe* it. What we can know is that the *Idea* of God is an Idea of Pure Reason.

SOCRATES: And are you saying that perhaps the world does not really exist either?

KANT: I am saying that the unified whole that we perceive may not exist that way—unperceived, as a thing-in-itself. I am saying that we cannot know that either.

SOCRATES: And you say that even the self does not exist in that way either?

KANT: That also.

SOCRATES: I go back to Descartes' argument then: "I think, therefore I exist." If I do not exist, then who is doing all this thinking? Might I be a figment of the Devil's imagination?

KANT: Ah, Descartes' "evil genius".

SOCRATES: Yes. How do you know this is not so?

KANT: I do not know it. I believe it.

SOCRATES: So the self is as problematic as God.

KANT: As impossible to *know*, yes. All I can know is what I call "the empirical ego", the self I find by introspection. But who or what is doing the introspecting? There is always a subject transcendent to any object, in all human knowing. And since it is not an object, it is not an object of knowledge. In other words, it cannot be known.

SOCRATES: Alas, if I had known that, I could have avoided the whole task of my life, to philosophize, which I summarized as the task "know thyself".

KANT: Are you jesting again, Socrates?

SOCRATES: Yes, Immanuel, I am. I realize you are not saying that there really *is* no self.

KANT: In fact, I am saying the opposite: that there is more, not less, in the self than reason can know; that beyond the "empirical ego" lies "the transcendental ego", which is in principle unknowable.

SOCRATES: As with "things in themselves", how can you know of it if it is unknowable?

KANT: My answer to this apparent contradiction is to make a distinction. These three ideas are not *constitutive* ideas but *regulative* ideas. They are not mental objects that have knowable definition, content, and substance. Their function is not to inform but to structure, not to fill our thought but to form it; not to expand our thought but to limit it. They are active ideas, acts-of-forming ideas, rather than passive ideas. They are not objects of thought.

SOCRATES: I understand. In other words, they are like computer hardware rather than computer software. They cannot be called up onto the computer screen.

KANT: What are computers?

SOCRATES: Oh, excuse me; I should not have used that analogy. I forgot that you did not have computers in your world.

KANT: The point, independent of all analogies and images, is that these ideas are not objects of thought but ways of thinking.

SOCRATES: But you have just made them objects of thought: first of all, by thinking them; and, in the second place, by defining them as not objects of thought; and also, in the third place, in defining them as world, self, and God rather than anything else.

KANT: I see your point. This *seems* self-contradictory. But it is not. When we say there is a field of objects, the field is not one of those objects. Yet in another sense the field *is* the object of our second thought and speech when we say there *is* a field that transcends its objects and is not one of those objects.

SOCRATES: Then in this second thought, the "field", which was *transcendental* in the first thought, becomes a *transcendent*, pre-"Copernican revolution" metaphysical object—which you say is impossible. But . . . but . . .

KANT: Why, Socrates, you look ill. Are there diseases in this world?

SOCRATES: It's only in my head. As I fear your whole world is. I think my inner computer may have caught a virus from your book.

KANT: What should we do about it?

SOCRATES: I think we should stop thinking about *The Critique of Pure Reason*, if that is where I caught my virus. Let us rest awhile and then begin our conversation about your other, more readable book, the *Grounding for the Metaphysics of Morals*.

10

The Single, Simple
Purpose and Point of the
Grounding for the
Metaphysics of Morals

SOCRATES: This little book of yours has become a philosophical classic, the most famous book about ethics since Aristotle.

KANT: I am quite honestly surprised by that.

SOCRATES: Why?

KANT: It is only a tiny, thin, short little book.

SOCRATES: Did you ever consider the possibility that that might have been precisely the reason for its popularity?

KANT: But the style is not easy and popular. It is the same style as my longer, more complete books.

SOCRATES: Did you ever consider the possibility that readers ignored your style, or endured your style and forgave your style, for the sake of the content and its importance?

KANT: But the content is simply a multistage argument that is sustained throughout the whole book, in an essentially linear fashion. You can summarize the book in ten or twenty consecutive points.

SOCRATES: Did you ever consider the possibility that that is another part of the reason for its popularity, its simplicity and directness of movement?

KANT: But it is not a complete moral philosophy. Its purpose is very modest, very narrow. As I wrote in the Preface, **"The present _Grounding_ is . . . intended for nothing more than seeking out and establishing the supreme principle of morality. This constitutes by itself a task which is complete in its purpose and should be kept separate from every other moral inquiry."**

G 392

SOCRATES: Did you ever consider the possibility that that might have been the strongest reason of all for its popularity?

KANT: It is possible, yes. And perhaps another reason is the _purity_ of the content, the purity of the moral philosophy that I teach in it.

SOCRATES: What do you mean by that?

KANT: I explained that also in my Preface as part of my purpose. I said that **"there is the utmost necessity for working out for once a pure moral philosophy that is wholly cleared of everything which can only be empirical and can only belong to anthropology."**

G 389

SOCRATES: Did you ever consider the possibility that that very "purity" which you saw as its main virtue is precisely the feature that most readers found questionable in it?

KANT: Oh, yes, I can understand that. People want to ground morality in some anthropology, some theory of human nature, something they experience, something empirical. But I ground it in pure reason. And that is hard for most people to grasp. The abstract is always harder than the concrete. So this is not an *easy* ethics to understand and to believe, much less to live. But the concepts of pure reason—things like mathematical and logical principles—are more infallible and unarguable and necessary and absolute than anything concrete that we meet in experience.

That is why I insist that **"the ground of obligation here must . . . be sought not in the nature of man nor in the circumstances of the world in** Ibid. **which man is placed, but must be sought a priori solely in the concepts of pure reason. . . ."**

SOCRATES: So you do not base your ethics on human nature, and on the nature of the deed done, and on whether the nature of the deed done conforms to human nature, as Aristotle did.

KANT: Right.

SOCRATES: Nor on situations and circumstances in the world, which are always changing, as moral relativists do: those philosophers who will be called utilitarians and pragmatists.

KANT: Right again.

SOCRATES: Nor do you base your ethics on all three factors, like St. Augustine and St. Thomas, who say that there are three moral determinants, three factors that make a deed morally good or evil: the nature of the act itself, and the circumstances, and the motive.

KANT: No, I concentrate on the motive only as the factor that distinguishes moral good from moral evil. As I say in my very first sentence after the Preface, the only thing that is good in itself is a good will. And I say soon after that that a good will is good only when it wills for a moral motive, when it is moved by moral duty.

SOCRATES: I see what you mean by the "purity" of your philosophy. Some would regard that as a virtue, others as a vice.

KANT: I say it is a virtue. And I say it is a vice to have more than one ground for moral obligation.

SOCRATES: So you would not agree with Aquinas, who would say that there are really no less than *five* grounds for moral obligation, the ultimate ground of moral obligation being the being of God, or the nature of God, or the character of God; *and also* the reason and mind and wisdom and self-knowledge of God, which follows His being; *and also* the will of God, which follows His reason; *and also* the nature of man, which is known and designed and created by God in His image; *and also* human reason, which knows these things when it is "right reason".

KANT: No, I would certainly *not* agree with that. It is a needlessly complex answer to a simple question.

SOCRATES: Some people would call the singleness of your answer a virtue, but others would call it a vice. They would call it oversimplification.

KANT: That is because they start out not with the simple, single concept of *obligation* but with the complex content of *the good*.

SOCRATES: But they would argue that the concept of obligation makes no sense unless it is relative to the good—that we are obligated to do something only because it is good, and obligated to avoid something only because it is evil.

KANT: I say they have it backwards. I say the good is relative to moral obligation.

SOCRATES: But you too begin with the good, in your very first sentence.

KANT: Yes, I *begin* with the concept of the good, but then I narrow it down: first to a good will, then to a will that has the right motive, which is moral duty, or respect for moral law; and then I narrow it even further, like a microscope increasing its magnification and decreasing its field—and finally I find the single supreme principle of morality, which I call the "categorical imperative", which is to ethics what the law of noncontradiction is to logic.

SOCRATES: Can you explain that parallel?

KANT: Yes. In both cases the supreme principle is the most supremely abstract and universal one, which does not come from experience, such as the experience of human nature or human circumstances in the world, but from pure reason. It is purely formal, not material.

SOCRATES: Can you explain what you mean by that distinction?

KANT: Yes. In logic, what makes an argument logically valid is not the content, or matter, but only the form. The same must be true in ethics.

Consider the following two arguments: "All men are mortal, and I am a man, therefore I am mortal." Compare, "All pigs are gods, and I am a pig, therefore I am a god." The content of the first argument is all true, while the content of the second argument is all false. Yet they both have the same valid logical form.

Or consider these two arguments: "All dogs are animals, and all dachshunds are animals, therefore all dachshunds are dogs." Compare "All pigs are gods, and all men are gods, therefore all pigs are men." The first of these two arguments contains nothing but truth, and the second nothing but untruth; but both are logically invalid because both have the same logical form. It is the abstract logical form of an argument that makes it valid, not the concrete content or matter.

It is the *form* that is absolute, universal, necessary, and certain rather than the content. Or rather, to put it more exactly, all of logic resolves back into the one and only absolutely absolute absolute, which is the law of noncontradiction, the law that tells us which logical forms are valid and which are not.

This is what I am seeking in ethics: the one absolutely absolute absolute.

SOCRATES: Perhaps I am going out on a limb, but I suspect that you may be a moral absolutist, then, yes?

KANT: Yes. Why do you smile? Oh, I'm sorry; I missed the dimension of subtle humor in your question.

SOCRATES: That remark itself is more subtly humorous than mine. Congratulations.

So you are searching for the north pole of morality, if you don't mind my use of a concrete image rather than your usual abstractions.

KANT: It is more like the pole star: the immovable standard for judging all motion. And this is why I seek an a priori ground for morality rather than grounding it in human nature, which is known only a posteriori, known only by experience. Only an a priori morality can be absolute.

SOCRATES: It seems that your *demand* for an a priori absolute is itself a priori and absolute. And this puts you into a logical dilemma, it seems: Can you justify this demand or not? If not, it seems merely arbitrary and personal. If so, if you can somehow prove it by some premise or justify it by some principle or standard, then *that* premise or standard would be the true absolute.

KANT: I do not derive it, or prove it, or justify the moral absolute from anything that is not absolute. That would indeed be logically self-contradictory, as your dilemma shows. But it is not arbitrary and irrational either. I escape your dilemma in the same way a logician escapes the same dilemma about the law of noncontradiction. I cannot and do not derive it from anything even more absolute, for there is nothing more absolute than the absolute; but it is not arbitrary either. It is the touchstone of rationality itself. What I call the "categorical imperative" is to practical reason what the law of noncontradiction is to theoretical reason.

SOCRATES: Suppose someone disagreed with that? What could you say to him?

KANT: They can't.

SOCRATES: They *can't?*

KANT: No.

SOCRATES: Why not?

KANT: Because it is self-evident.

SOCRATES: To everyone?

KANT: Yes. We all know it, deep down, insofar as we are rational. It is simply impossible to doubt the law of noncontradiction. We can *say* we doubt it, but we lie. For all meaningful expressions of doubt of the law of noncontradiction, and all meaningful expressions of doubt of anything at all, and in fact all meaningful expressions of anything at all, in order to be meaningful, must presuppose the law of noncontradiction. To say "I doubt the law of noncontradiction" you must assume that doubting the law is not the same as *not* doubting that law. Otherwise, when you say "I doubt the law of noncontradiction" you mean "I do *not* doubt the law of noncontradiction." So whether you doubt it or not, in both cases you do not doubt it.

SOCRATES: That certainly seems to be an unanswerable argument. And now you say that there is a parallel in ethics, an ethical law of noncontradiction, so to speak? And that you will be the first polar explorer to reach this pole?

KANT: I say that the pole must exist, but I do not say that I am the first to reach it. I say that we *all* reach it, that we all know this moral absolute, deep down, just as we all know the law of noncontradiction.

SOCRATES: What about moral relativists, who deny that there *is* any moral absolute?

KANT: Moral relativism is not an inferior kind of morality; it is not morality at all. And we all know that: we all know that *moral* obligation is a different *kind* of thing from merely social obligation, the obligations of social conventions, or the practical, pragmatic, utilitarian need to do certain things or to avoid certain things. We do not feel moral guilt when we break merely social conventions, or when we fail in merely practical things. If there is moral obligation at all, it is absolutely binding.

SOCRATES: And you want to explore where the rope that binds us comes from.

KANT: Yes. It is a great mystery, this binding. It is as if this rope came down from the sky and yet did not fall. Morality binds us without the use of physical force, whether forces outside us, like the police, or forces inside us, like animal desires and instincts. Morality does not push us, as instincts do, from ourselves. It pulls us, so to speak, and the pull comes from itself to us. I want to explore that pull, that obligation.

SOCRATES: So the experience of moral obligation is your data, and your ethics is an attempt to explain that data.

KANT: That is one way to put it, yes.

SOCRATES: You seek, then, a theory of the moral absolute to explain and justify the experience of absolute obligation?

KANT: Yes.

SOCRATES: Suppose someone simply denies that data, that experience of being under moral obligation? Suppose someone denies the existence of any obligation that is not merely social or conventional or pragmatic?

KANT: No man can do that if he is aware of himself and honest with himself.

SOCRATES: But many people do *not* believe that. Moral relativists do not believe that.

KANT: I say they really do. As I say in my Preface,

Ibid.   **That there must be such a** [pure, a priori, and absolute moral] **philosophy is evident from the common idea of duty and of moral laws. Everyone must admit that if a law is to be morally valid, i.e., is to be valid as a ground of obligation, then it must carry with it absolute necessity.**

SOCRATES: So you say that *everyone* knows that morality is absolute, and that moral relativism is not morality at all?

KANT: Yes.

SOCRATES: How would you answer those who disagree with *that*?

KANT: I would ask them to read my book and then refute my argument there after they have seen it. I think that would be better than arguing about the issue before reading the book, in the abstract, in a vacuum.

SOCRATES: Fair enough. So the fundamental purpose of the book is . . . ?

KANT: To find and formulate "**the** [one] **supreme** G 392 **principle of morality**". To find "**the ground of** [moral] **obligation**".

SOCRATES: So the data at the beginning, the data you are trying to explain, or to "ground", is the experience of moral obligation.

KANT: Yes.

SOCRATES: So if a person simply has no such experience, he has no data and could not follow your argument.

KANT: That is true. But no such person exists. All persons, that is, all rational beings, have that power, the power to have that experience of obligation. This is true even for nonhuman persons, persons with nonhuman bodies, if they exist on other planets, and or even for persons with no bodies at all, pure spirits like angels, if they exist.

SOCRATES: I think I understand your quest. So now let us follow your journey.

II

The Starting Point:
A Good Will

SOCRATES: Here is the very first sentence of your
G 393   book: "There is no possibility of thinking of anything at all in the world, or even out of it, which
can be regarded as good without qualification, except a *good will.*"

Why all the qualifications? Why not simply say
"The only thing good without qualification is a good
will"?

KANT: I say "no *possibility*", not just "no actuality",
and I say "no possibility of *thinking* of anything . . .",
not just "no possibility of *discovering* anything . . .",
and I say "anything at all in the world *or even out of
it*", to show that this is an a priori. It is not dependent on experience. It is necessary and universal. It is
necessary because it is not contingent upon anything
else, and it is universal because there is no possible
exception to it.

SOCRATES: So if you have found this, you have found
your moral absolute. The moral absolute is a good
will. Your quest is over. You are finished. The book
only needs to be one sentence long. Your end is your
beginning.

KANT: No. I am looking for the pole star, remember, not the pole. My first sentence gives you the pole, the human pole, the thing in man that is good-in-itself, and the only such thing. But I have not yet found what *makes* it good: its standard, its rule, its law. I have found the thing morality judges: human wills. I have found the one who is in the dock, but I have not yet found the one who is on the Judge's bench.

SOCRATES: Most people would say that that is God, the absolutely good Being, at the ontological root of absolute moral law.

KANT: I do not deny the existence of God, but I do not rest my morality on the existence of God.

SOCRATES: So you do not believe the statement that "if God does not exist, then everything is permissible."

KANT: I do not. Just as the law of noncontradiction is a law that binds the minds of everyone—both monists and pluralists, materialists and spiritualists, atheists and theists, dogmatists and skeptics, nominalists and realists—so the moral absolute binds the wills of everyone, including atheists and theists. By the way, was it an atheist or a theist who uttered that statement?

SOCRATES: It was first uttered by a famous nineteenth-century theist named Dostoyevski and then quoted approvingly by a famous twentieth-century atheist named Sartre.

KANT: And I will wager that the theist used it to prove the existence of God from the premise of the existence of moral absolutes, while the atheist used it to prove the nonexistence of moral absolutes from the premise of the nonexistence of God. Am I right?

SOCRATES: You are uncannily right, Emmanuel.

KANT: See? Bringing God into the picture does not solve the problem at all.

SOCRATES: It does if God's existence can be either proved or disproved.

KANT: But it cannot be proved or disproved. And I think half of humanity agrees with me here. And an absolute morality should not be convincing to only half of humanity.

SOCRATES: I see your point. It is a point of strategy, or method, rather than a point of substance, of what is in fact true.

KANT: I am glad you understand my strategy. Both atheists and theists often do not understand that and insist that their ethics be based on either the existence of God or the nonexistence of God. That is like demanding that the rules of logic be based on the existence or nonexistence of Platonic Ideas. That would make it binding only on Platonists, or only on anti-Platonists. It would not be universal. But morality is universally binding. Therefore I cannot base it on God's existence, even if He does exist, or on His nonexistence, even if He does not exist.

SOCRATES: But suppose God in fact does exist, and suppose that the moral law does in fact bind us because God willed it, and suppose that we know the moral law and its bindingness only because our moral conscience is the voice of God in our souls.

KANT: Suppose that is so. What then?

SOCRATES: Would your moral system, which does not base morality on God, still hold then if in fact the real basis of morality is in fact God?

KANT: Indeed it would. Let me give you a parallel case. Suppose that God does in fact exist, and suppose that the universe exists only because God created it, and suppose that our reason can know the universe only because our reason is part of the image of God in us, our participation in the mind of God. This is what theists believe. Suppose this is all true. Would it then follow that science must assume theism? That science would not work, or that the scientific method would be invalid, if the scientist believed in atheism?

SOCRATES: No.

KANT: Why not?

SOCRATES: Because even if God is the ultimate cause of both the universe and human reason, one can know the effect without knowing the cause.

KANT: Exactly. And the case in ethics is parallel. Even if the pole star of ethics which I seek is in fact derived from God, nevertheless one can know it, and know its absolute authority, and one can navigate by it, whether or not one believes there is a God behind it.

SOCRATES: The parallel seems to work.

KANT: And the practical strategy too. For an ethic that depends on religious faith cannot be universal. It would divide mankind and contribute to religious war rather than to peace. But a universal ethic based on reason alone would foster unity rather than division, just as the universal use of the scientific method and the laws of scientific logic has fostered agreement and cooperation in science, and the settling of disputes that for all previous ages were unsettled.

SOCRATES: I see. That is why God is not your starting point, even though you believe God exists.

KANT: Yes.

SOCRATES: So God does not come into your ethics at all, then?

KANT: He does, but at the end rather than at the beginning. I do not reason from God to morality but from morality to God. And even then I do not claim that morality proves the existence of God. I know that not everyone will agree with my theistic conclusion, but I think everyone will agree with my moral starting point.

SOCRATES: And your starting point is that the only thing good in itself is a good will?

KANT: Yes.

SOCRATES: Can you prove that point?

KANT: Not by deducing it from prior premises, no. But I can explain it so clearly that I can convince everyone that it is true, simply by appealing to universal moral common sense. That is what I do in the next few sentences.

SOCRATES: We had better investigate them, then. You mention four other kinds of good, and for each of them you deny that it is good in itself, as a good will is; and you say that what makes them good is a good will; and you say that if there is not a good will, these four things are *not* good, at least not morally good:

> [1] **Intelligence, wit, judgment, and whatever** G 393
> **talents of the mind one might want to name**
> **are doubtless in many respects good and de-**
> **sirable, [2] as are such qualities of temper-**
> **ament as courage, resolution, perseverance.**
> **But they can also become extremely bad and**
> **harmful if the will, which is to make use of**
> **these gifts of nature and which in its special**
> **constitution is called character, is not good.**
> **[3] The same holds with gifts of fortune;**
> **power, riches, honor, even health, [4] and**
> **that complete well-being and contentment**
> **with one's condition which is called happi-**
> **ness make for pride and often hereby even**
> **arrogance, unless there is a good will. . . .**
> **The sight of a being who is not graced by**
> **any touch of a pure and good will but who**
> **yet enjoys an uninterrupted prosperity can**
> **never delight a rational and impartial spec-**
> **tator.**

KANT: Do you think this is too simplistic a judgment, Socrates?

SOCRATES: No, for I think it is the judgment of humanity. It is not a radically new discovery or invention on your part. For instance, St. Thomas Aquinas teaches essentially the same thing: "He who has a will is said to be good so far as he has a good will; because it is by our will that we employ whatever powers we may have. Hence a man is said to be good, not by his good understanding, but by his good will" (*Summa Theologica*, I, 5, 4 ad 3).

KANT: So you agree with my starting point, at least. You agree with this "judgment of humanity".

SOCRATES: Yes, but I wonder how you prove it. Do you simply *assume* that humanity is right here? Aren't you trying to *prove* each step of your argument? Isn't your ethics supposed to be a purely rational and critical one, an appeal to "pure reason" rather than experience?

KANT: Not in Descartes' sense, no. I do not begin with universal doubt, as he does. I do not exclude everything but "clear and distinct ideas". I do not demand purely logical deductions of each step, as Spinoza did. I do not do ethics "in the mode of geometry."

SOCRATES: Hmm . . . you seem to take the "critical problem", the demand for proof, much more seriously in epistemology than in ethics.

KANT: But I do appeal to pure reason rather than to culturally or historically changeable experience. I appeal, in fact, to universal moral experience. And since all men share this experience, I think it is often sufficient merely to analyze and explain rather than to prove.

SOCRATES: But suppose someone did disagree with your analysis.

KANT: Disagree with what? Why might they disagree with what I say here?

SOCRATES: They might say that you mislabel courage, resolution, and perseverance as "qualities of temperament", gifts of nature, when in fact they are moral habits built up out of many morally right choices. They might say that just as we are responsible for our choices, we are also responsible for our character, which is the sum of our habits, both good and bad, both virtues and vices, for our habits are gradually formed by our choices. If this is true, then those habits too are good or bad in themselves. Yet you say they are not, that they are only instruments that are made good or bad by a good will, which is the only thing that is good in itself. You thus reduce "character" to a mere "quality of temperament", which seems to be merely a set of inborn psychological tendencies that are merely inner gifts of fortune.

KANT: But it is certainly true that we are not personally responsible for gifts of fortune, including our bodily qualities, and even to some extent our emotional qualities that are caused by our bodily qualities, such as a native intelligence, or a hot temper, or a predisposition to alcoholism caused by the chemistry of the brain.

SOCRATES: That is true. And therefore we do not properly praise or blame people for these gifts of fortune, do we?

KANT: No.

SOCRATES: But we do properly praise people for their courage, resolution, and perseverance, don't we?

KANT: Yes.

SOCRATES: You see what follows, then.

KANT: That these are not merely gifts of fortune.

SOCRATES: Exactly. And therefore that you misclassified them.

KANT: How do you classify them?

SOCRATES: Clearly, they are moral virtues, which are good habits which in turn are caused by repeated choices. And since the person is responsible for his choices, he is also responsible for his virtues and vices.

KANT: I do not deny that. It is just not part of what I am trying to do in this book, which is to find the single absolute moral principle that is a priori and certain, not to develop a complete ethic based on true but less than certain a posteriori data from some theory of human nature, either philosophical anthropology or scientific anthropology or psychology.

SOCRATES: I see. But I think the judgment of humanity, or moral common sense, would disagree with another classification that you make in this passage, namely, the way you label or classify "happiness". This too you remove from the area of morality, as you did to "qualities of temperament" like courage, perseverance, and resolution. You say that happiness

is simply the satisfaction of all our inclinations, don't
you?

KANT: Yes.

SOCRATES: But that is only *contentment*.

KANT: How would you distinguish happiness from
contentment?

SOCRATES: Contentment is purely subjective, purely
psychological. A moral monster could be quite content with his moral monstrosities. But happiness—
eudaimonia, makarios, "blessedness"—has also an objective dimension in Aristotle and the ancients gener-
ally. It means moral perfection, like the perfection of
a good work of art. And therefore it can include suffering, as a necessary means of moral training on the
road to perfection. But contentment cannot include
suffering; it is the opposite of suffering. And therefore it must be a mistranslation to translate *makarios* as "happy". It results in the absurdity of making
Jesus say "Happy are you who mourn."

KANT: These are very fundamental issues, and it would
take a long time to sort out and understand them.
When you speak of moral common sense and the
"judgment of humanity", you are thinking most typ-
ically of the ethics of Aristotle, are you not?

SOCRATES: Yes.

KANT: But Aristotle was doing a very different *kind*
of ethics than I do. That is why he began with the
concept of *happiness* while I begin with the concept of
a good will. He was looking for the supreme *end*, the

"summum bonum", while I am looking for the *good-in-itself*. His ethics was teleological and ontological. It was based on metaphysics and anthropology, on what is, and on what is in human nature. Mine is not ontological, but deontological.

SOCRATES: But why?

KANT: Because there are deep-seated disagreements about ontology, or metaphysics, and also about anthropology. But there are no disagreements about the law of noncontradiction. I am trying to find the fundamental principle of agreement, the moral law of noncontradiction, so to speak, so that my ethics can be a universal ethics for all rational beings, not just an ethics for those who believe in a certain philosophy of being and a certain philosophy of man.

SOCRATES: I see. And would it therefore logically follow that many of the apparent contradictions between you and Aristotle may well be only apparent rather than real, if they are taken out of this context, the context of what kind of ethics you are doing and what you hope to attain by your ethical systems? Is that what you say?

KANT: Perhaps. I would have to look at each apparent contradiction by itself. I think there are some real contradictions between us, even after provision is made for misunderstanding due to ignoring our different contexts and purposes.

SOCRATES: This is a very important question, for the two of you are the two most influential ethical philosophers in history. And yet I think we do not have time to investigate that question now in any way that would do justice to it, for we are supposed to be examining *your* book, not Aristotle's.

Yet let me ask you just one question to open that road of investigation, even though we do not have time to travel very far along it. What is your evaluation of the famous saying of Aristotle's greatest disciple, St. Thomas Aquinas, when he says in his *Summa Theologica* (I-II, 34, a 4) that a man is good when his will loves the good, and evil when his will loves the evil, and hence the things we love tell us what we are?

KANT: In the first place, I agree with him that what makes a man good or evil is his will, rather than any of those other things I mentioned: all the gifts of nature or of fortune, even temperament. For they are merely raw material to be used well or badly according to the good or bad choices of the will.

But, on the other hand, I disagree with him when he says that a will is good only because it wills the things that are good in themselves. I do not believe that there are any things that are good in themselves, except a good will.

SOCRATES: Do you also disagree with him when he says that the difference between good and evil is determined by love?

KANT: No, because he clearly means by "love" an act of the will rather than a feeling or a mere desire. Confusing love with a feeling is a very common confusion, and a very debilitating one. The will is free;

feelings are not. Love is an act of his free choice, over which a man has control and therefore responsibility. It is not, as with the animals, a mere instinct or desire that is not free and therefore not something for which the "lover" is personally responsible.

As I say a little later on in my book,

G 399   **Undoubtedly in this way also are to be understood those passages of Scripture which command us to love our neighbor and even our enemy. For love as an inclination cannot be commanded; but beneficence from duty, when no inclination impels us and even when a natural and unconquerable aversion opposes such beneficence, is practical . . . love. Such love resides in the will and not in the propensities of feeling, in principles of action and not in tender sympathy; and only this practical love can be commanded.**

SOCRATES: So you would say that a man with instincts or propensities or inclinations within him that are bad or selfish or harmful or unnatural—for instance, someone with an appetite for eating human flesh, to take an extreme and unusual case—you would say that such a man is doing moral evil when he *chooses* to actually eat another man's flesh, but *not* when he simply discovers in himself this terrible appetite.

KANT: Correct. What he chooses to *do* about this desire is a matter of his free choice. Having the desire to begin with is not.

SOCRATES: Would you also include *thinking* under the category of "doing"?

KANT: Yes, insofar as his thoughts are under the command of his will. For instance, if he chooses to deliberately think more and more about eating human flesh, and to fantasize about its pleasures, *that* thinking can rightly be judged as morally bad because it is commanded by his will. But simply having this unnatural desire in himself, or having thoughts of cannibalism rise up in his mind involuntarily, against his will, does not yet make him immoral, any more than discovering that he has an inordinate fear of pain makes him a coward. Only his choice to refuse to risk pain makes him a coward.

SOCRATES: The same would apply to sexual desires as any other desires, then.

KANT: Yes.

SOCRATES: And also homosexual desires?

KANT: Yes. It is one thing to say that they are *unnatural*, or psychologically unhealthy. That may be so, as most of humanity has always believed. But it is quite another thing to say that these desires as such are *immoral*. That is a confusion. No desires are immoral if they are not commanded by the will, because nothing is immoral if it is not under the control of the will. But choosing to *act* on these desires is under the control of the will and therefore may be moral or immoral.

SOCRATES: So you would say, then, that even if homosexual desires are unnatural and unhealthy, someone who has them can still be a morally good person, even a saint, if he does not act according to these desires?

KANT: Yes. And the same is true of heterosexuals. If their desires are promiscuous, as they often are, and if that is unhealthy, as most of humanity believes it is, they can still be morally good persons, even saints, if they do not act according to those desires.

SOCRATES: What of the commandment not to lust, not to covet one's neighbor's wife? That seems to make the desire itself morally evil.

KANT: What is commanded must be deliberate. Even God cannot command an inclination. That is an impossibility based on a confusion, and God does not command impossibilities, nor are His commandments based on confusions. So if lust is immoral, it must be more than an inclination. It must be a choice.

SOCRATES: I think you are more in agreement with Aquinas, and even with Aristotle, than it seems on this point.

However, you seem to be in disagreement on the other point; you still do not accept that whole other dimension of ethics, as they do: the material content, the belief that some things by their very nature are good and others evil—for instance, the things defined by the Ten Commandments. And therefore you do not define a good will as a will that chooses to will the things commanded by these Commandments (or any other set of commandments), or a bad will as one that chooses to will the things forbidden by them.

KANT: You are right there, Socrates. I do not base my ethics on metaphysics.

SOCRATES: And does that fact stem from your epistemology in your *Critique of Pure Reason*, which we have already examined at such painful length?

KANT: It does indeed.

SOCRATES: Especially on your denial that our reason has access to things in themselves.

KANT: Yes.

SOCRATES: Including things like human nature and the nature of specific human actions.

KANT: Yes.

SOCRATES: So in your epistemology, all that is left for theoretical reason is the knowledge of appearances. And how could you base an absolutistic ethics on the knowledge of mere appearances?

KANT: You understand my predicament rightly. But yet I do base ethics on reason, on practical reason rather than theoretical reason. I believe I have discovered the self-justifying axiom of practical reason in this little book. That is what my "categorical imperative" is. So I do not need to do metaphysics in order to do ethics.

SOCRATES: Thank you for explaining that point so clearly. We may want to return to that point later, after we have explored your whole book. For it seems questionable to most people. They would say that ethics *must* be based on some kind of metaphysics— that whether anything is morally *commanded or forbidden* depends on whether it is *good or evil*, and whether it *is* good or evil depends on *what it is*, on its real nature, and therefore that we must be able to know the real nature of things if we are to have ethics at all. So they would say that your epistemology undermines the foundation for ethics.

KANT: How ironic! How can this be? My whole strategy is to do exactly the opposite: to provide a surer foundation for ethics. The epistemology is there for the sake of the ethics.

SOCRATES: So your epistemology justifies your ethics?

KANT: No, it is my ethics that justifies my epistemology rather than vice versa. I demolished the inadequate and questionable foundations for the ethical house, the foundations in speculative, transcendent metaphysics, only in order to establish that house on a much firmer foundation. Instead of borrowing an alien foundation from metaphysics, I establish the ethical building on an ethical foundation. *That* was my deepest motive for my epistemology. It was not merely to solve the epistemological puzzles of David Hume; it was for ethics.

SOCRATES: So the investigation we are doing now, into your ethics, is really an investigation into the ultimate point and purpose of your epistemology.

KANT: Yes.

SOCRATES: So no one can fully understand the importance of your *Critique of Pure Reason* without understanding your ethics, and the relation between these two.

KANT: In the last analysis, this is true.

SOCRATES: This is a subtle point of strategy that is not explicitly stated in either of those two books. And thus it can be missed by readers of either or both of them.

KANT: The point can be missed, but I did state it. For instance, I said, I have cleared away reason to make   CPR way for faith.   B xxx

SOCRATES: I thank you for making that subtle point so clear.

12

What Makes a Good Will Good?
Duty Versus Inclination

SOCRATES: After this long tangent, let us return to the beginning of your book. You have established your "Archimedean point", the fulcrum of your whole system, or the premise of your whole many-step argument: that the only intrinsic good is a good will. Let us see what your next move is, your second step.

KANT: Here it is:

G 394 **A good will is good not because of what it effects or accomplishes, nor because of its fitness to attain some proposed end; it is good only through its willing, i.e., it is good in itself. When it is considered in itself, then it is to be esteemed very much higher than anything which it might ever bring about merely in order to favor some inclination, or even the sum total of all inclinations.**

SOCRATES: This point would seem to follow from your first one. If a good will is the absolute and intrinsic good, then it cannot be good only for some relative or extrinsic good, as a means to that end, nor can it be judged by that standard.

KANT: That is my logic.

SOCRATES: Does this mean that my will that you attain happiness is not a good will because it wills something other than a good will?

KANT: No. It means that your will to my happiness is a good will not because it attains its end and makes me happy, but because it is a good will in and of itself. This is clear if we consider a bad will and compare a bad *will* with bad *results*. Everyone knows that *attempted* killing is morally worse than *accidental* killing, even though the *result* is not as bad. (In attempted murder, the other person lives; in accidental killing, he dies.) You see? Everyone knows that the good or bad will is not made good or bad by the result but by itself, by its very act of willing rather than by its success in attaining what it wills.

SOCRATES: Do you regard this second point as uncontroversial, then? Would no one disagree with it?

KANT: Only those who do not believe there is any intrinsic good, or moral absolute, at all. I think my second point here would be agreed to even by those who say that something like the Ten Commandments defines the difference between a good will and a bad one, by those who say that what makes a will good is not the mere willing but the objects willed. They too would have to agree that the *essence* of being a good person—of being a very good person, of being a saint—is a good will. Although they would add other factors also, they would say this is the essence. That is clear from their judgment of intended killing as morally worse than accidental killing.

SOCRATES: I see. I think most people would agree with you so far.

Your next point—or perhaps it is only a definition of what you mean by *this* point—is the meaning of "duty". You say:

G 397   **The concept of a will estimable in itself and good without regard to any further end must now be developed. This concept already dwells in the natural sound understanding and needs not so much to be taught as merely to be elucidated. It always holds first place in estimating the total worth of our actions and constitutes the condition of all the rest. Therefore, we shall take up the concept of *duty*. . . .**

KANT: It could be called a third point, though it emerges simply from an understanding of my second point. I would summarize it this way: that an act must be done from the motive of moral duty in order to have any moral worth.

SOCRATES: So you say two things here: first, that what makes an act morally good is its *motive*, and, second, that duty is what makes a motive a morally good motive.

KANT: Yes.

SOCRATES: You realize, I'm sure, that most moralists would disagree with the first of these two points. They would say that at least *three* things make an act morally good or evil: the motive, the nature of the act itself, and the situation or the circumstances, including the foreseen consequences of the act.

KANT: I realize that.

SOCRATES: You eliminate these other two factors from your moral calculation.

KANT: Yes.

SOCRATES: Why?

KANT: Because they are uncertain.

The nature of the act itself is uncertain because it presupposes metaphysics. It presupposes that we can know the nature of things as they are in themselves. And that is a questionable assumption. I do not want to base my morality on any questionable assumptions.

And the situation, or the circumstances, or the consequences are even more obviously uncertain. They are empirical and depend on accurate and complete observation of the whole situation, or the larger situation, including all the consequences of the act. And this is impossible for any merely human mind.

SOCRATES: You assume, then, that moral calculation of good and evil cannot be based on anything uncertain or merely probable.

KANT: Not if we want an absolutist ethics rather than a relativist one.

SOCRATES: And that is why it must be wholly a priori?

KANT: Yes.

SOCRATES: And that is why you call such an ethic "pure" and "cleared of anything empirical"?

KANT: Yes.

SOCRATES: You realize, of course, that that feature of your ethics, which you deem its highest virtue, will be deemed its greatest vice by many of your critics. And these critics will be not merely the moral relativists, who say that morality is relative to changing circumstances and probable calculation of consequences, but also moral absolutists like the disciples of Aristotle and Aquinas, who insist that morality must be based on human nature and a "natural law" that can be known by reason.

KANT: I realize that. My strategy is to bypass all questionable or controversial assumptions, and to admit only the necessary and the universal, which are not questionable or controversial.

SOCRATES: How similar to Descartes you are! You demand an ethics of "clear and distinct ideas".

KANT: I do not deny that other factors should be taken into consideration in making moral decisions, especially a knowledge of human nature and of situations. But this can only be probable knowledge. In this book I am searching for the single moral absolute, the principle of all principles. And that must be absolutely certain, and therefore a priori rather than a posteriori, based on pure reason rather than on experience. Readers who interpret my *Grounding* as claiming to put forth a complete ethical system are radically misunderstanding me, and quite inexcusably so, for in my Preface I made that point quite clearly —that this book is only about one thing: the single supreme principle of morality. It is not about anything else, or how much else there is.

SOCRATES: Does this mean that you do not deny that the other two moral factors can influence the moral goodness or evil of an act? Do you mean to say that an act is good or evil *only* because of its motive and not at all because of its object—the thing that is willed —or because of the circumstances?

KANT: I do not deny that they play a role. For instance, I do not deny that it is right to do what is in itself just or charitable or merciful or helpful, and wrong to do what is in itself unjust or cruel or harmful. Nor do I deny that the same act may be right in some circumstances and wrong in others. But I say that I can deduce the same conclusions, the same moral map, so to speak, and make the same moral discriminations, the same lists of good and evil actions, from my single principle, which I call the "categorical imperative", as they can from their many principles such as the Ten Commandments or any list of various virtues and vices.

SOCRATES: I see. That claim remains to be tested, of course, since we have not yet found your single "categorical imperative".

KANT: Yes.

SOCRATES: Let us then go on to your next point. . . .

KANT: I think before we go on we should be sure we understand the exact point I make about duty: that duty is a matter of the right *motive* for the will rather than a matter of the object or content of what is willed.

SOCRATES: I agree: we need to be sure we understand this distinction very clearly. And here is your explanation, and your first example:

G 398   [T]o preserve one's life is a duty; and, furthermore, everyone has also an immediate inclination to do so. But on this account the often anxious care taken by most men for it has no intrinsic [moral] worth. . . . They preserve their lives, to be sure, in accordance with duty, but not from duty.

How do you distinguish doing it *"in accordance with* duty" from doing it *"from* duty"?

KANT: Doing it "in accordance with duty" means doing whatever things duty commands, whether from the motive of duty or not. Doing it "from duty" means doing it from the motive of duty.

SOCRATES: Whether it is the things duty commands or not? Does it make no difference what things I do?

KANT: Of course it does. But the motive will take care of the things. For if I have the motive of obeying my duty, I will try to do the things duty commands. If I do not do the things duty commands but I still have the motive of obeying my duty, then the only reason I do not do the things duty commands is because I am ignorant or mistaken about what things these are. But ignorance is not a moral fault. It is an intellectual fault.

SOCRATES: I see. To complete your example of preserving one's own life, you go on then to say:

On the other hand, if adversity and hopeless   Ibid.
sorrow have completely taken away the taste
for life, if an unfortunate man . . . wishes for
death and yet preserves his life . . . not from
inclination or fear, but from duty — then his
maxim [principle] **indeed has a moral content.**

And then you add a second example: the example
of being beneficent or generous:

To be beneficent where one can is a duty;   G 398
and besides this, there are many persons who
are so sympathetically constituted that . . .
they find an inner pleasure in spreading joy
around them. . . . But I maintain that in such
a case an action of this kind, however dutiful
and amiable it may be, has nevertheless no
true moral worth. It is on a level with such
actions as arise from other inclinations. . . .

You do not mean to say that inclination as such
is *evil*, do you? Or that acting out of inclination is
always evil?

KANT: Of course not. Inclinations are neutral. They
are raw material.

SOCRATES: Do you say that it is more morally praise-
worthy to do your duty when you have no inclination
to do so, or when your inclinations run contrary to
your duty?

KANT: I do. For then the will has no crutch and must
will its duty with all its might.

SOCRATES: That seems rather severe. Are you saying, then, that an act is morally good only insofar as it hurts? Most people will not agree with that, I think.

KANT: Yes, I am saying that, but I think that most people *will* agree with it. They admire a deed much more when it is difficult than when it is easy. That is why the willingness to sacrifice, and the willingness to endure the suffering it brings, is universally regarded as the surest sign of a saint.

SOCRATES: But is it not also true that *joy* in doing good is the surest sign of a saint? The Catholic Church will not canonize a saint unless she finds in his life "heroic joy" as well as heroic suffering.

KANT: That may be true, but the joy is the fruit, not the motive. And I think the Church teaches that also. I think there is no difference in judgment between the ethics of Immanuel Kant and the ethics of ordinary people, or of the Church, as far as which moral judgments are made. The only difference is not our conclusions but our premises, I mean the principles that are used to make the moral judgments. My principles are fewer—only one—and more a priori—not based on experience—and therefore more certain.

SOCRATES: I wonder. I seem to see a difference also in the judgments you make. Let's take a concrete example. Suppose a saint and a notorious sinner confront the same temptation. Suppose St. Francis of Assisi and Bluebeard the pirate are walking together alone at night and they see a collapsed bank vault with a fortune in gold spilled out onto the street. Suppose Bluebeard, for once in his life, resists the temptation to steal other men's gold and passes the gold by.

St. Francis also passes it by, for he has no temptation at all to steal the gold, for he is a saint, and wise, and has no foolish lust or greed for gold. Do you say that there is more moral goodness in Bluebeard than there is in St. Francis at that moment when both choose to pass by and not to take the gold?

KANT: I cannot answer that question simply, because it is really two different questions that are confused. You ask me to judge the two *acts*, the two deeds, the two choices. You also ask me to judge the two *men*. I say there is much more moral worth in Bluebeard's choice than in Francis', because it is harder and relies more on free will and not on inclination. But I also would say that Francis' inclinations are better, that is, more helpful to morality, than Bluebeard's. Francis has trained his inclinations well, like good servants, so that he does not have to do all the work himself. And I do not deny that this is a good thing to do. I only say that all the moral worth resides in the act of choice itself, not in any of its consequences, even the consequence of having morally helpful inclinations, good habits.

SOCRATES: I see. So you seem to say that even though the moral choice begets good inclinations, these children of moral choice, so to speak, are not moral children. You say they are not so much *begotten* as *made*. For the products of human making are not human, but the products of human begetting are.

KANT: You could put it that way.

SOCRATES: Hmmm. . . . Perhaps if you had married and had children you would have put it in a different way, for you would have seen things in a different way.

KANT: You are arguing from an analogy, Socrates.

SOCRATES: No, for I am not arguing at all. I am musing.

KANT: Musing?

SOCRATES: Yes. You might try it some time. It might improve your philosophy.

KANT: How?

SOCRATES: When you muse, you see some things that you might not see when your thinking is directed and controlled only by your reason and will.

KANT: What do you say I fail to see?

SOCRATES: You fail to see any intrinsic moral quality in inclinations, or desires, or habits, at all. For you they are merely *instruments* for moral goodness, like crutches that help you to walk more easily.

KANT: That is correct.

SOCRATES: Duty is the central concept in your whole ethics, is it not?

KANT: Yes.

SOCRATES: Not "good", or "end", or "happiness", or "blessedness", or even "God".

KANT: No. Duty.

SOCRATES: You probably do not realize this, but there are two unfortunate emotional connotations of the word "duty" that will make it very difficult for English-speaking readers centuries after your death to appreciate or embrace your point about the centrality of duty. One of them is the fact that "duty" sounds like "doo doo", which is the word their mothers used for excrement when they were toilet trained. The other is the fact that the German war criminals that were tried for murdering six million innocent noncombatants after history's most horrific war, a war that engulfed the entire world, all defended their actions by saying that they were "doing their duty".

KANT: It should be obvious that what I mean by duty has nothing to do with obeying the immoral commands of a cruel tyrant. It has nothing to do with obeying the commands of any man, good or evil, in war or peace. It is the relation of a will to the moral law, not to another human being.

SOCRATES: Is "duty", then, the same as "obligation"?

KANT: You might say that duty is the *cause*, or explanation, of obligation. *Because* we bound by duty, we experience obligation. Because our will, or practical reason, is in that relation to the moral law which we call duty, we experience obligation.

SOCRATES: So the moral law is like a hinge of a pendulum, and obligation is like the ball of the pendulum, and duty is like the arm that rivets the ball to the hinge.

KANT: Something like that, yes.

SOCRATES: So if obligation is the data, and duty is the hypothesis that explains the data, and the categorical imperative is the hypothesis that explains duty.

KANT: You could put it that way, yes.

SOCRATES: Where, then, does the concept of the "end" or goal come in?

KANT: My ethic is not a teleological ethic but a duty ethic. You might say that the difference is in the prepositions. Mine is not an ethic whose central image is that of a man walking down a road *toward* a goal. It is an ethic whose central image is that of a man *under* orders, under law. It is not an ethic that looks forward, or "onward", to joy or sanctity or Heaven, at the forecasted consequences in this world or in the next, but an ethic that looks backward, so to speak, at my duty, at my maxim, at my principle.

SOCRATES: Those would seem to be two dimensions of every complete ethic. Why did you confine yourself to the duty dimension only and explicitly exclude the teleological dimension, the dimension of end and purpose?

KANT: Because I wanted to find the pole star, the ethical absolute. And that cannot be happiness, or any other end, because happiness is uncertain, and because it varies for different people, and because it is not obligatory. It is merely an ideal, a goal that you may strive for, and that you naturally do strive for, and that you are led to strive for and are motivated to strive for, but you are not *obligated* to strive for. There is nothing morally absolute about it. It is not universal and necessary. It is not a priori. I explained later in my book why happiness cannot be the *summum bonum*, the greatest good, as Aristotle and Aquinas take it to be:

G 418   [T]he concept of happiness is such an in-
            determinate one that even though everyone
            wishes to attain happiness, yet he can never

say definitely and consistently what it is that
he really wishes and wills. The reason for
this is that all the elements belonging to
the concept of happiness are unexception-
ally empirical, i.e., they must be borrowed
from experience, while for the idea of happiness there is required an absolute whole, a
maximum of well-being in my present and in
every future condition. Now it is impossible
for the most insightful and at the same time
most powerful, but nonetheless finite, being
to frame here a determinate concept of what
it is that he really wills. Does he want riches?
How much anxiety, envy, and intrigue might
he not thereby bring down upon his own
head! Or knowledge and insight? Perhaps
these might only give him an eye that much
sharper for revealing that much more dread-
fully evils which are at present hidden but are
yet unavoidable, or such an eye might burden
him with still further needs for the desires
which already concern him enough. Or long
life? Who guarantees that it would not be a
long misery? Or health at least? How often
has infirmity of the body kept one from ex-
cesses into which perfect health would have
allowed him to fall, and so on? In brief, he is
not able on any principle to determine with
complete certainty what will make him truly
happy, because to do so would require omni-
science. Therefore, one cannot act according to determinate principles in order to be
happy. . . .

SOCRATES: Might not one still act on *faith* in order to be happy?

KANT: Faith? How could faith make us happy? What faith?

SOCRATES: Simply what Christians mean by faith. Faith that there is a God Who is, in the first place, omniscient and Who knows all the "determinate principles" that we do not know that would make us maximally happy; faith in a God Who, in the second place, is good and Who loves us with the love of beneficence, or charity, and thus wills our maximum happiness; and faith in a God Who, in the third place, is omnipotent and thus able to perform all that He wills.

KANT: That could indeed constitute a man's faith—I would call it hope, since its object is the future—but it would still not answer my philosophical question. It might make a man happy but it could not define the moral good. No concept of happiness in the human mind can do that. No concept of happiness is sufficiently certain to be the pole star, for any ethics that needs an absolute as distinct from uncertain and always changing relativities.

SOCRATES: Do you see all teleological ethics as being less than absolute?

KANT: Yes. I wanted, above all, to refute ethical relativism, which I saw arising in my day largely from the philosophy of David Hume, and which I saw as a kind of infection that would poison all human activity with a fake but soothing substitute for morality if it ever became established orthodoxy in any society.

SOCRATES: Perhaps you were prophetic in your diagnosis there. But perhaps you were unnecessarily narrow in your prescription. Surely there are *other* alternatives to ethical relativism that are still teleological?

KANT: For instance?

SOCRATES: For instance, Plato.

KANT: No, not even Plato. He too has only a hypothetical imperative: *if* you want to be happy, you must be good. Plato's *Republic* has that as its central theme: that justice is always more *profitable* than injustice, more productive of happiness. That is a prudential imperative, a pragmatic imperative. It is not an ethical imperative. It is not truly absolute. That is not the pole star.

SOCRATES: What about an ethic like Aquinas', where the pole star is God?

KANT: Even then. *If* you want God, you must be good. That is still a hypothetical imperative.

SOCRATES: I suspect that if Aquinas were here he would agree with your "categorical imperative" but also with his own teleology. They seem to be two dimensions of his ethic that are so well integrated, like body and soul, that no one noticed any gap or tension between them until you first came up with your purely nonteleological ethics. Does that not suggest to you that you are doing something like pulling the soul out of the body?

KANT: No, it does not suggest that to me. For I do not do ethics by a tour through the history of philosophy and a comparison of different systems, like works of

art, judging them by the standard of completeness.
I do ethics by reason, by beginning with data that
everyone knows and accepts and then reasoning to
the necessary conditions of possibility for this data.

SOCRATES: What if it results in a system that ignores
part of the human data?

KANT: What human data are you thinking of?

G 397 SOCRATES: You claim your concept of duty **"already
dwells in the natural sound understanding and
needs not so much to be taught as merely to be
elucidated"**, do you not?

KANT: Yes.

SOCRATES: Would you say, then, that the understanding that ranks duty less than the morally highest thing
is not a sound understanding?

KANT: I would.

SOCRATES: But from my observation of human beings, I would say that the vast majority of human
beings are in that category in their thinking about
morality.

KANT: Why do you say that?

SOCRATES: Because the vast majority would rank *love*
far above duty in moral worth. They would say that it
is a mother's love for her child, rather than her sense
of duty to the moral law, that leads her to sacrifice
for her child, and that that is right and proper and
high and holy. They would say that generosity to the
poor done out of genuine love for the poor is of a
higher moral quality than generosity done only out
of duty. They would say that duty is not the highest

but the lowest of truly moral motives, that we fall back on it when other motives fail, like warriors retreating to a castle keep. They would say that duty is the last bulwark against doing evil rather than the highest motive for doing good.

Do you say that these people are wrong?

KANT: No. Obviously this common judgment of mankind is not simply wrong. But I think you are confusing two different questions in comparing my ethic of duty with their ethic of love. My question is not the concrete question: What is a saint? What is the best human being? What is a morally perfect person? And what is the relation between the motives of duty and charity in such a saintly person? My question is merely the abstract question: What is the essential defining formula of morality itself?

SOCRATES: You do *not* say, then, that the person who is motivated by love rather than duty is morally inferior to the person who is motivated by duty rather than love? That the husband who answers his wife's question Why are you faithful to me? by saying that he wills to do his duty—you do not say that this man is a morally better man than the husband who answers, truthfully, that he loves his wife?

KANT: Of course not. But these two things cannot fairly be compared. One is abstract, one concrete.

SOCRATES: But they are both possible motives for concrete persons to have in concrete situations. And so they *can* be compared.

KANT: And here is how I compare them. If the love is merely animal instinct, mere inclination, then it is *not* as high and as moral a motive as duty. If on the other hand the love is beneficence, charity, the will to the good of the other, then it cannot be contrasted to duty because it is identical with duty! For my duty to my spouse is precisely to love her with the love of beneficence, or unselfish charity.

SOCRATES: How then would you explain acts that are heroic, acts that we label "beyond the call of duty"? For instance, sacrificing your life for your friend?

KANT: They are heroic acts of beneficence. What do you see in them that you think I cannot explain?

SOCRATES: Do you deny that they are morally good?

KANT: Of course not.

SOCRATES: But you say morality is coterminous with duty.

KANT: Yes, in its essence and definition.

SOCRATES: Then you must say that these heroic acts are acts of duty rather than acts that go beyond the call of duty. In that case, you make heroic acts moral duties. And that is both theoretically and practically impossible.

It is theoretically impossible because you then identify contrary terms: acts beyond the call of duty and acts done from duty.

It is practically impossible because you then put a terrible burden of moral obligation upon all men —to act not just from duty but beyond the call of duty—a burden that even a saint could barely bear, and a burden that conscience does not admit. For we do not feel guilt for failing to act beyond the call of duty, but for failing to do our duty. We do not feel guilt for not going beyond what the moral law commands; we feel guilt for not obeying what the moral law commands.

KANT: Perhaps we *should* feel guilt for not going beyond the call of duty. But, in any case, I will admit that I misspoke, Socrates: moral goodness is *not* simply coterminous with duty. Of *course* there is a distinction between acts that are merely doing our duty and acts that go beyond our duty. Both kinds of acts are free of all moral taint; but while the first kind are limited to what is commanded by duty, the second kind are even better than that and indeed do "go beyond the call of duty". I could not disagree with moral common sense and deny that.

SOCRATES: But then duty is the lowest thing, not the highest thing, in morality. It is the minimum, the fall-back position.

KANT: Let it be so, then. Duty is only the minimum. But it is the essence of the minimum, and that is the essence of morality, for the essence of anything is its minimum, not its maximum, as having three sides and three angles is the essence of a triangle, not having three large sides; and as having a body and a soul is the essence of a man, not having a healthy body and a saintly soul. So duty is only the minimum, but it is the essence, and I have identified the essence.

13

The Call for Purity of Motive

SOCRATES: Your next step is to define duty. You say,
G 400 **"Duty is the** [moral] **necessity of an action done out of respect for the** [moral] **law."** Could you put that in more ordinary language?

KANT: Yes. Duty is the motive that binds the will to moral obligation to obey the moral law.

SOCRATES: I do not see anything controversial here.
G 402 But then you ask: **"But what sort of law can that be?"** And you answer: **"Law as such."** Why do you say that?

KANT: I explained that in my Preface. I seek the essential form of morality rather than the particular content. An essential definition cannot give particular examples. That is why no set of particular laws, like the Ten Commandments, however right and holy they may be, can be the very essence of morality. The essence is single, while particular moral laws are many.

SOCRATES: That would seem to be obvious to anyone who has studied logic.
Next, you *formulate* this one essential law as fol-
G 402 lows: **"I should never act except in such a way that**

I can also will that my maxim [subjective principle of willing] **should become a universal law** [for all men]."

And this, finally, is your famous "categorical imperative" in its first formulation.

KANT: Yes. And this concludes the first section of my book.

SOCRATES: I wonder why it does not conclude your whole book. You have found your north star, have you not?

KANT: Yes, but I must still prove it, test it, apply it, and deepen the understanding of it by formulating it in two other ways. And that is what I do in the rest of the book.

SOCRATES: Let us proceed to that then.

KANT: The first thing I do is answer three objections to what I have already said about duty. The first objection is based on a misunderstanding of my purpose and method in this book. My method was to begin with universally accessible data, which anyone can check in his own moral experience. But that does not mean that I have derived the concept of duty from experience. I say: **"If we have so far drawn** G 406 **our concept of duty from the ordinary use of our practical reason, one is by no means to infer that we have treated it as a concept of experience."**

It is essential to understand my strategy here. My argument is purely a priori, not a posteriori. That is why the following objection, though it is true, does not refute me: because it arises from experience. It is an a posteriori truth, and it does not refute my a priori truth:

Ibid.   **On the contrary, when we pay attention to our experience of the way human beings act, we meet frequent and — as we ourselves admit — justified complaints that there cannot be cited a single certain example of the disposition to act from pure duty. . . . Hence there have always been philosophers who have absolutely denied the reality of this disposition in human actions and have ascribed everything to a more or less refined self-love.**

SOCRATES: You are thinking here of moral cynics like Machiavelli and Hobbes?

KANT: Yes. And less radical versions of them.

SOCRATES: And how do you refute them?

KANT: Not empirically! They have launched an empirical, psychological attack on my a priori argument. That is like trying to refute a mathematical equation with an experiment in a laboratory. Thus I say:

Ibid.   **Yet in so doing they have not cast doubt upon the rightness of the concept of morality. Rather, they have spoken with sincere regret as to the frailty and impurity of human nature, which they think is noble enough to take as its precept an idea so worthy of respect but yet is too weak to follow this idea. . . .**

You see, a universal and necessary concept or precept cannot be refuted by a particular and contingent sense experience because it is not a generalization that is derived from particular and contingent sense experiences.

SOCRATES: Not even by abstraction?

KANT: Not even by abstraction. And even if you *could* derive universal *concepts*, like human nature, or squareness, or greenness, from the sensory experience of particular instances of them—from your experience of particular human beings, or square things, or green things, as Aristotle claims we do—even then you still could never derive *precepts* from sensory experience. Even if much observation of human beings brings us closer to a knowledge of universal human nature, no amount of observation of human behavior can bring us even the tiniest bit closer to a knowledge of duty and moral law. It is another *dimension*. It's as impossible as adding width to a line simply by adding length. No amount of data about what *does* happen tells us anything at all about what *ought* to happen. You cannot derive an "ought" from a mere "is", any more than you can derive a color from black and white, or time from space, or spirit and consciousness from mere matter. It is another whole *dimension*, a *metabasis eis allo genos*, a "going-over-into-another-*genus*", as Aristotle would say.

SOCRATES: In other words, my fear or respect of some wild animal that could kill me is an altogether different *kind* of fear or respect from my fear or respect for the moral law. Is that what you say?

KANT: Exactly. And I think each of us can verify this if only we listen to all aspects of our experience, inward as well as outward. Experience teaches us the difference between nonmoral fear and moral fear, and thus between a morality that is based only on nonmoral fear, like Hobbes' morality, which is based on the fear of violent death, and a morality that is based on moral fear, on respect for moral law, like my morality.

SOCRATES: I see. In that sense, the distinction between the morality that is *not* derived from experience and a pseudomorality that *is* derived from experience is itself derived from experience.

KANT: Yes, but only if your concept of "experience" includes *moral* experience, the experience of being under moral law and obligated to do our duty. But I would not call that "experience" at all because it is a priori.

SOCRATES: By a priori you mean merely that it is prior to *sense* experience.

KANT: Yes. The moral law is a standard we bring to sense experience, and which we use to judge what we experience. When we see one man kill another, we judge this as morally wrong, by standards that we do not derive from that experience as we derive our knowledge of colors and shapes and events from experience.

SOCRATES: Can you prove that we do not derive the law from experience?

KANT: Easily. For the law is our standard of judgment, and the standard could not be both prior to the experience it judges and also posterior to it.

SOCRATES: But in a larger sense, "experience" includes not only sense experience but also moral experience: the experience of something like a Platonic Idea of justice. We seem to discover this, rather than creating it. We seem to bump up against it with our will as our bodies bump up against walls and our mind bumps up against logical and mathematical truths.

KANT: That is what seems to be the case. I maintain that in all three cases we are deceived. As I showed in my epistemology, we create the forms that we seem to discover, both the forms of sense perception, space and time, and the forms of abstract thought, the categories. And when we get to the end of this book and to the third and final formulation of the categorical imperative, we will find that we do the same thing with our will: we create the moral law, we will it into being, we ourselves are the law makers, as we ourselves are the meaning makers.

SOCRATES: In both cases it seems you have man usurping the role of God. It would seem that this philosophy would fit a humanist and atheist better than a Christian and a theist.

But since that is probably your most controversial point, and since it comes up explicitly only at the end of your book, let us defer our investigation of it for now and return to your second objection. What is it? I did not notice any explicit listing of three objections here in your text.

KANT: It is implicit. The objection is that we seem to learn morality from experience because we learn it from concrete examples. Plato, you remember, began his *Meno* by asking whether virtue (1) could be taught (as he believed) or whether (2) we get it in some other way: by practice (as Aristotle believed), or (3) by nature, innately (as Rousseau believed), or (4) in some other way, perhaps by force and contrary to our nature (as Hobbes believed). Most people would reply with a fifth answer: that we learn morality from concrete examples, from moral heroes. Children learn morality from their parents' example, and Jesus' disciples learn morality from the example of Jesus.

SOCRATES: And you disagree with this popular opinion?

KANT: I do. The answer has a grain of truth to it, but it confuses *learning* morality with *being encouraged* to be moral. Before any encouragement for being morally good can possibly come to us from concrete examples in our experience, a posteriori, we must already have an a priori concept of what it is to be morally good. We must know what the examples are examples *of* in order for us to use them as examples. That is simply a logically self-evident point, not one that can be disputed. It does not depend on anything in human nature or psychology.

G 408   That is why I say: **"Worse service cannot be rendered morality than that an attempt be made to derive it from examples."**

SOCRATES: That is a shocking statement!

KANT: Wait. I explain it and justify it by a very simple logical argument:

Ibid.   **For every example of morality presented to me must itself first be judged according to**

principles of morality in order to see whether it is fit to serve as an original example, i.e., as a model. But in no way can it authoritatively furnish the concept of morality. Even the Holy One of the gospel must first be compared with our ideal of moral perfection before he is recognized as such. Even he says of himself, "Why do you call me (whom you see) good? None is good (the archetype of the good) except God only (whom you do not see)."

SOCRATES: Your point here is purely logical, then? It does not depend on your theological beliefs about the identity of Jesus?

KANT: No. I just used Jesus as an example.

SOCRATES: But then you go on to say that **"imitation has no place at all in moral matters."** That seems rather extreme, doesn't it? And isn't it refuted by experience? Surely having good examples and models and heroes makes a great difference to us? Surely children with good parents are more likely to be good than children with bad parents? Do you deny this? G 409

KANT: Of course not. The "moral matters" I speak of here means the quest for a definition of morality, not the encouragement to live more morally. That is why I go on to explain that **"examples serve only for encouragement."** Being encouraged to be moral presupposes that we already know what being moral means, and therefore it cannot be the *source* of that knowledge. As I have said repeatedly, moral knowledge is a priori. Ibid.

SOCRATES: But even though we cannot *derive* or *deduce* morality from examples, we can still *teach* it by examples, can't we?

KANT: Only if you mean by "teaching" *encouraging* the student to practice what he already knows—not if you mean by "teaching" the first deriving of that knowledge.

SOCRATES: Can't we teach morality as we teach logic?

KANT: What do you mean?

SOCRATES: You would agree that the knowledge of both is a priori, and that every rational being has the innate ability to understand both, would you not?

KANT: Yes, indeed.

SOCRATES: And yet we teach logic. So we can also teach morality—not in the same way we teach a posteriori subjects like history, but by a kind of reminding and clarifying of what is already implicitly known. Something like what Plato called *anamnesis*, remembering an innate knowledge.

KANT: It is known a priori, yes. And teaching it is therefore reminding the student of what he already implicitly or unconsciously knows. I grant that.

SOCRATES: All right, what is your third objection?

KANT: That objection too is implicit rather than explicit, implied rather than stated. It is that my standard of a pure motive is too high to be practical.

SOCRATES: And what is your answer to it?

KANT: That it is simply not true. It *is* practical. I say that

> **the pure thought of duty and of the moral**   G
> **law generally, unmixed with any extraneous**   410-11
> **addition of empirical inducements, has . . .**
> **an influence on the human heart so much**
> **more powerful than all other incentives which**
> **may be derived from the empirical field that**
> **reason in the consciousness of its dignity de-**
> **spises such incentives.**

SOCRATES: In other words, "Do it because it's the right thing to do" moves us more powerfully than "Do it because if you do, I will reward you with things you desire."

KANT: Yes. That is exactly what I claim.

SOCRATES: I am intrigued by the difference between this answer and your other two answers. You answered the first two objections, which came from the empirical order, or experience, by an answer that was wholly on the a priori theoretical order. But you answer this third objection, which also comes from the order of experience, on that very same level.

KANT: I do.

SOCRATES: So you claim that moral idealism is not only the correct ideal a priori; it is also the most practical, the most workable appeal in practice, a posteriori, in experience, even to us weak and impurely motivated mortals.

KANT: I do.

SOCRATES: That seems to imply a very high and idealistic view of mankind.

KANT: Yes. That does not make it untrue.

SOCRATES: I did not mean to imply that it did.

KANT: My point here is not merely to appeal to a sentiment or feeling of optimism or mere idealism. My claim is that in the real world, moral idealism actually works better in practice than moral compromise. I say that "do it because it's right" moves moral agents (and all men are moral agents) more than "do it because I will give you rewards," which is how we move animals when we train them.

In a footnote I mention being asked

G 411, n. 2 **why it is that moral instruction accomplishes so little.**

My answer . . . is just that the teachers themselves have not purified their concepts: since they try to do too well by looking everywhere for motives for being morally good, they spoil the medicine by trying to make it really strong. For the most ordinary observation shows that when a righteous act is represented as being done with a steadfast soul and sundered from all view to any advantage in this or another world, and even under the greatest temptations of need or allurement, it far surpasses and eclipses any similar action that was in the least affected by any extraneous incentive; it elevates the soul and inspires the wish to be able to act

in this way. Even moderately young children feel this impression, and duties should never be represented to them in any other way.

SOCRATES: So you say we should not try to make moral duties more attractive by adding rewards to them?

KANT: That is exactly what I say. Even children admire someone who simply does the right thing because it is right more than someone who does it as a means to the end of getting a reward.

SOCRATES: Even if the reward is Heaven?

KANT: Especially if the reward is Heaven!

SOCRATES: But didn't God do exactly that according to your Bible? Aren't there many promises of rewards in Heaven for being good on earth?

KANT: No indeed. God's first lesson to His chosen people was not that "You must be holy because I have the power to make you rich", or that "You must be holy because I have all the pleasures you want and I will give them to you only if you are holy." He said, instead, "You must be holy because I the Lord your God am holy."

SOCRATES: That is true, according to your records. But there are *also* promises of rewards: prosperity and success and triumph over their enemies.

KANT: Yes, but these are deliberately ambiguous. Do they refer to worldly success or spiritual success? Triumph over the armies of pagan nations or over the armies of evil in the soul? The ambiguous promises have to be interpreted, and this tests the hearts of the interpreters.

In fact, according to those records, which we Christians call the Old Testament, God so carefully trained His chosen people in pure morality that He did not clearly reveal to them the existence of Heavenly rewards, or of Heaven, or of life after death, for many centuries. He trained them in the right motive first, so that when the Heavenly rewards were finally revealed, much later, in the later prophets and in the New Testament, it would not corrupt them and would be a gift rather than a bribe.

SOCRATES: I see. But once the rewards were revealed, why was it not a "bribe" then?

KANT: What kind of reward would it be if God had to bribe us to be morally good by offering us something other than the moral good as our reward in Heaven? Suppose He had said to us, "I know your heart is really set on pleasure rather than goodness, and that is all right with me; but I have the power to give you pleasure or to withhold it eternally, so you must obey Me in order to get these pleasures, not because you love Me for what I am, not because you love that which I am—perfect moral goodness—but only because I hold the power." What motive would that appeal to?

SOCRATES: I see your point. That would appeal to the worship of power, not goodness, and to the fear of pain and the love of pleasure rather than the fear of evil and the love of goodness.

KANT: And that would elicit the groveling of a syco-phant to a tyrant. And if *that* is the God to Whom a man offers worship and obedience, I think the true God rejects that worship and even that obedience.

Look at the saints, the truly holy people, whose hearts are purest: the thing they look forward to the most in Heaven is not the absence of pain but the absence of sin. How could a pleasure-monger enjoy such a Heaven, one that takes its nature from God, and thus is the country of saints, the country of moral goodness? How could such a Heaven be the fulfill-ment of their deepest desire if their deepest desire was not for goodness but for pleasure?

SOCRATES: I cannot quarrel with your theology. But I would like to return to your morality.

KANT: Fine.

SOCRATES: You want to purify morality from the lure of rewards and the fear of punishment.

KANT: Yes.

SOCRATES: But surely there are two very different kinds of rewards. One of them is a natural and intrin-sic reward. For instance, peace is a proper and natural and intrinsic reward for a soldier fighting a just war, and therefore his desire for this reward is moral and proper and not mercenary. And marriage is a natural and intrinsic and proper reward for courtship, and a man's desire to marry a woman is not selfish and mercenary. But the desire for money is a corrupting reward for either war or love. For money is not the intrinsic, natural reward of either war or love. So we judge a mercenary soldier or a mercenary lover as a morally compromised man. But we do not judge a man who longs for the reward of peace or the reward of marriage as morally compromised.

And thus a Heaven of material pleasures would be an impure reward for moral virtue; but a Heaven of virtue, or "the communion of saints", would be a pure and proper reward for it, just as marriage is the proper reward of courtship.

And the same would apply to punishments. A Hell that punished spiritual sin by physical pains would be impure and improper, but a Hell that consisted in the natural and inevitable results of sin—loneliness and despair and the absence of light—would be a proper punishment. Indeed, as Plato argued in the *Republic*, virtue is its own reward and vice is its own punishment.

KANT: I agree with Plato's point there. And I do not deny your distinction between proper and improper rewards. But this distinction comes from empirical experience and thus does not form part of my argument in this book. Again I remind you: I am only seeking the single a priori essence of morality, not the many pieces of concrete psychological wisdom that you speak of. Once you understand my purpose, there is no contradiction between us.

SOCRATES: I am not testing your philosophy by mine, but by what I believe to be moral common sense.

KANT: Then I maintain that there is no contradiction between my philosophy and moral common sense—

especially in my main point, which you have not gotten to yet, my "categorical imperative".

SOCRATES: Well, then, I think we are ready to look at that.

14

The First Formulation of
the Categorical Imperative:
The "Golden Rule"

SOCRATES: What you do next is very logical. (1) First, you define "imperative", (2) then "categorical", and (3) then explain what the "categorical imperative" is: that it is formal rather than material and a priori rather than a posteriori. (4) Only then do you formulate the categorical imperative. (5) Finally, you claim that it is universal, that all other moral imperatives can be derived from it. So if I have understood your strategy and outline correctly, those should be our next five topics.

KANT: You have understood correctly.

SOCRATES: First, then, you define an "imperative" as follows: **"All imperatives are expressed by an *ought* and thereby indicate the relation of an objective law of reason to a will that is not necessarily determined by this law."** I think we should be sure we are not misunderstanding any of your key terms in this definition.

First of all, the term "imperative" usually is a *gram-*

matical term, indicating a certain kind of *sentence*. But for you it is something real, is it not?

KANT: Yes. It is the reality designated by an imperative sentence—by some imperative sentences, at least. (I don't want to say that "Please pass the salt" is the same kind of imperative as "Thou shalt not kill.")

SOCRATES: An imperative is a kind of judgment, is it not?

KANT: Yes.

SOCRATES: And all judgments intend something, or refer to something, or point to something, or designate something, do they not?

KANT: Yes.

SOCRATES: So what is the reality designated by an imperative?

KANT: It is not a *thing* or *substance* but a *relation*. It is neither something outside the will nor something *in* the will, but the *relation* between a law and a will.

SOCRATES: I see.

KANT: And that relation is **"expressed by an *ought*"**.

SOCRATES: When you say it is "expressed", do you mean an imperative is simply a linguistic "expression" rather than a reality?

KANT: No, it is a reality—if I understand your distinction. How would you distinguish a reality from a linguistic expression?

SOCRATES: I would say that we can be wrong about reality but we cannot be wrong about linguistic expressions, because we are the sole authors and arbiters of linguistic expressions, but we are not the sole authors and arbiters of reality.

KANT: I will agree to that.

SOCRATES: Notice that I said "*sole* authors" rather than "authors" simply, because according to your "Copernican revolution" we *are* authors of reality —of its form, but not its matter.

KANT: And form, or essence, or nature, is universal and necessary rather than individual and contingent. That is why there is only one set of forms for all minds. But languages are not universal or necessary but individual and contingent. That is why there are many languages.

SOCRATES: I see. By the way, how dependent on your epistemology in the *Critique of Pure Reason* did you intend the your ethics in *Grounding for the Metaphysics of Morals* to be?

KANT: I tried to keep this book free from overt dependence on the *Critique of Pure Reason*. So I am happy with your attempt to keep the language neutral on that controversial epistemological issue of the "Copernican revolution". For I suspect that many more readers will agree with my ethics than with my epistemology. I claimed that my ethics is nothing more than what **"already dwells in the natural sound understanding and needs not so much to be taught as merely to be elucidated"**. But I never claimed that for my epistemology.

G 397

SOCRATES: Thank you for clarifying that intention.

Your third point of the five we are investigating is that the relation between law and will is expressed by an *ought*.

You mean by this "ought" a real obligation rather than a mere subjective feeling, do you not?

KANT: Yes. A mere feeling is not an obligation, and it is certainly not an obligation to a law that binds the will.

SOCRATES: And by "obligation" you mean essentially the same as "duty".

KANT: Yes.

SOCRATES: Now your fourth point: you call what the will is related to a "*law*", not a "value" or an "ideal" or a "good" or a "goal" or a "purpose" or an "aspiration". That seems to me quite important. For thinkers after you will prefer to use a term like "value" or "values" rather than that simple, hard term "law". "Law" sounds so unyielding and objective, like a rock.

KANT: That is precisely why I used it.

SOCRATES: And you mean by a "law" here not a generalization, like "the sun rises every day" or "matter attracts other matter."

KANT: Indeed not. For one thing, it is an imperative rather than an indicative. For another thing, it is not dependent on repeated sense experience. That is why I called it a "law of reason" rather than a "law of nature". The laws of nature are discovered by sense experience. They are a posteriori. Moral laws are a priori, like the laws of mathematics. That is why they are necessary and universal.

SOCRATES: But unlike the laws of mathematics, they tell us what ought to be rather than what is. Two plus two necessarily and universally *are* four, but men do not necessarily and universally obey the laws of morality.

KANT: But they necessarily and universally *ought* to.

SOCRATES: I understand. And this "ought" brings up a fifth feature of your definition: the point that a will that is obligated must be *free* rather than **"necessarily determined"**.

KANT: Yes. Most succinctly put, **"*ought* implies *can*."** Two plus two are not under any *obligation* to equal four, nor is matter under an *obligation* to attract other matter. And therefore there is no freedom in two plus two to choose to be or not to be four, or in matter to choose to attract or not to attract other matter.

SOCRATES: I think we have understood what you mean by an "imperative" then. Let us see what you mean by a "categorical" imperative.

This seems pretty clear. You say:

G 414   **Now all imperatives command either hypothetically or categorically. The former represent . . . a possible action as a means for attaining something else. . . . The categorical imperative would be one which represented an action as objectively [morally] necessary in itself, without reference to another end.**

A little later, you say the same thing in only slightly different words:

> **Now if the action would be good merely as**   Ibid.
> **a means to something else, then is the im-**
> **perative hypothetical. But if the action is**
> **represented as good in itself, and hence as**
> [morally] **necessary in a will which of itself**
> **conforms to** [moral] **reason as the principle**
> [motive] **of the will, then the imperative is**
> **categorical.**

So "Throw me a life preserver", "Guard your flanks when you attack the center", and "If you want to be loved by others, love them first" are hypothetical imperatives. But "Choose life" and "Do not start wars" and "Love your enemy" are categorical imperatives. Is that correct?

KANT: Yes.

SOCRATES: Plato made a similar distinction at the beginning of Book II of his *Republic*, when he had Glaucon complain that all other moralists had justified morality by merely hypothetical imperatives like "Be good if you want to be successful, or praised, or honored, or rewarded, whether by men in this life or by the gods in the next." But no one had shown that being just (which for Plato was the key moral virtue) was a good in itself; that "virtue is its own reward."

KANT: Yes, but even Plato went only halfway, so to speak, in justifying morality. Like me, he freed it from the taint of selfishness and greed for external rewards, whether given by gods in the next life or by men in this life. But he justified it by the internal reward of happiness. Justice, for him, was to the soul what health is to the body. So he still had a hypothetical imperative: "*If* you want to be happy, be moral." He did not see that the truly moral reason for being moral is simply to be moral! So for him virtue was not really its own reward. He purified morality somewhat, by detaching it from some rewards—external rewards. I purified morality even more, by detaching it from all rewards.

SOCRATES: Even from its own intrinsic, natural reward of happiness?

KANT: Even that.

SOCRATES: I wonder.

KANT: What do you wonder?

SOCRATES: I wonder why another "Emmanuel" seems to have disagreed with you, Emmanuel.

KANT: The Christ of the Gospels, you mean?

SOCRATES: Yes. If I read the Bible in light of your philosophy, I cannot help wondering why He was not as "enlightened" in His morality as you were.

KANT: The Divine Mercy condescends to human frailties. He tempers the wind to the shorn lamb. Many men do many good works for rewards. But the saints did not work for rewards.

SOCRATES: What did they work for? For duty rather than rewards?

KANT: If they were truly saints, yes.

SOCRATES: Hmmm . . . as I read them, they seem to have worked neither for duty nor for rewards but for love.

But let us return to your text. You next remind us of four features your "categorical imperative" must have. And these four characteristics of the categorical imperative are also characteristics of the law of noncontradiction in logic.

First, **"There is** [only] **one** [such] **imperative"** rather than many.

Second, **"It is not concerned with the matter of the action . . . but rather with the form."**   G 416

Third, **"It is not concerned with . . . its intended result, but rather with . . . the principle from which it follows."**

Fourth, it is **"entirely a priori".**   G 419

You seem to have set the bar very high in demanding such an imperative. You seek not just the polar continent but the pole itself.

KANT: Yes, but it is surprisingly easy to find. And once found and formulated, it is so obvious that everyone knows it is true. Everyone has already found this "pole" unconsciously. All I do is raise to consciousness, and to the level of explicit formulation, that which **"already dwells in the natural sound understanding".** It is simply what is popularly known as "The Golden Rule". Here is my formulation of it: **"There is only one categorical imperative and it**   G 421 **is this: Act only according to that maxim whereby you can at the same time will that it should become a universal law."**

SOCRATES: This is indeed the well-known "Golden Rule" that we find in the teachings of Moses, and Confucius, and Jesus, and many others. I think, however, that all three of them would say that the most universal moral rule is even more universal than this one: something like "Do good and not evil."

KANT: My rule is better because it is just as universal as "Do good and not evil" but it also has a feature that "Do good and not evil" does not have: it immediately and by itself alone determines all moral duties, without the addition of empirical premises that specify goods and evils, which can be questioned.

SOCRATES: What is wrong with arguing this way, as most other moral thinkers would do? The major premise is that everyone should always do good and not evil, and the minor premise is that stealing, for example, is not good but evil, and therefore the conclusion is that everyone always should not steal. Where is the weakness in that argument?

KANT: The weakness is in the minor premise. It needs to be proved. And it is my "categorical imperative" that proves it, proves that no one should steal, and proves it without relying on any other premises. So this other moral system really depends on my categorical imperative. On the other hand, my categorical imperative does not depend on the other moral system, for it works all by itself, without any other premises, even the two premises you mentioned.

SOCRATES: We must examine whether your categorical imperative is indeed just as universal as "Do good and not evil." Why do you think it is?

KANT: That's the reason it is called the *"Golden* Rule", Socrates.

SOCRATES: I thought that was because it is perfect and incorruptible, like gold.

KANT: True, but it's also because it is a universal touchstone for all other rules, as gold is the price of all other metals in the world's commerce. And also because all other moral rules can be derived from it or reduced to it, as in medieval alchemy all other metals could supposedly be transformed into gold. It is the universal imperative, so that, as I say next, **"all imperatives of duty can be derived from this one imperative."** And I then proceed to show how this is done, by four examples.   G 421

SOCRATES: Without going into detail and example, can you summarize how it is done? What is the general principle you find in all the examples?

KANT: In each of them, we find that

if we now attend to ourselves in any transgression of a duty, we find that we actually do not will that our maxim [principle] should become a universal law — because this is impossible for us — but rather that the opposite of this maxim should remain a law universally.   G 424

For example, when we murder, we do not want others to murder us, but we want others to obey the law "Thou shalt not murder." And when we steal from others, we do not want them to be free from the law "Thou shalt not steal" and steal back from us, because we would then no longer profit by our stealing. And when we lie to others, we do not want them to lie to us, because the purpose of a lie is to get an advantage over the other, so that we know the truth but they do not.

So the touchstone of every moral evil, every transgression of duty, is this contradiction in our will: we *cannot* will for ourselves what we will for others. We cannot will moral equality under a universal and exceptionless principle. We can only will some moral inequality, so that *we* need not obey the law, while others do need to obey it. Thus I say:

G 424   **We only take the liberty of making an exception to the law for ourselves (or just for this one time) to the advantage of our inclination. Consequently, if we weighed up everything from one and the same standpoint, namely, that of reason, we would find a contradiction in our own will, viz., that a certain principle be objectively necessary as a universal law** [for all] **and yet subjectively** [for me] **not hold universally but should admit of exceptions** [for myself].

We will at the same time an A proposition, "*All* men should obey the law", and an O proposition, "*Not* all men should obey the law, for *I* need not obey the law." That is as much a contradiction as any theoretical contradiction in logic.

So, you see, the categorical imperative is, first of all, a priori, not derived from experience, so that it is universal and necessary, with no exceptions or contingencies; in the second place, it binds by sheer force of logic, not by its specific matter or content; and third, it is a law of reason, not of inclination.

SOCRATES: There seem to be three touchstones here, or three dimensions of your single touchstone; and it seems that all three always give us the same result. First, all transgressions of duty make an exception for ourselves. Second, they all therefore involve contradictions in our will. Third, they all prioritize inclination over duty. That is their motive.

And all three touchstones always seem to give us the same result, the same label of "evil" attached to the same actions.

So your Golden Rule does seem to be all the things you claim for it.

KANT: That was short and sweet. I am glad to see that you understand how obvious this principle is.

SOCRATES: But we are not finished. I said that it *seems* to be all the things you claim for it, especially universality. But we may be wrong in that judgment. Many ideas seem to be what they are not. That is why we must keep investigating them. So let us test this test, or touch this touchstone, to see whether it really does hold up.

KANT: I'm sure it will.

SOCRATES: But I am not sure. That is why I keep questioning.

I cannot think of any evil action that is not accurately labeled by your principle. It does indeed seem that no evil action can be willed as a universal law.

And the reason for that seems to be the very nature of evil: it is, in a way, self-contradictory, as you say.

However, there seem to be many *good* acts, even acts that are morally obligatory for the actor, that could *not* become universal obligations. For instance, your own lifestyle of celibacy.

KANT: That is not a moral obligation but a following of my inclinations.

SOCRATES: But for a priest or a monk or a nun it would be a moral obligation. And for a soldier many things would be morally obligatory, and morally good, that are neither obligatory nor even good for others, such as taking care to learn learn to shoot and care for guns.

KANT: But we *can* will celibacy to be a universal law too—for all priests. And we *can* will that all soldiers learn to shoot and care for guns.

SOCRATES: Ah, but then we are making exceptions for certain classes of people. Even though individuals would still be wrong when they disobey the law for all priests, or all soldiers, yet the universality of the rule is not absolutely universal. If I will that all people *who are not priests* marry, I might just as well will that all people *as smart as I am* be allowed to lie, or all people *as poor as I am* be allowed to steal. We have abandoned your categorical imperative once we start making exceptions for anyone, whether an individual or a group, and whether the group is an institution, like the priesthood or the army, or whether it is simply the group of all smart people or all poor people. I might will that anyone in my particular embarrassing predicament may lie to get out of that particular predicament, and thus justify myself for lying.

So it seems that your "categorical imperative" is indeed a negative universal but not a positive universal.

KANT: Socrates, instead of directly defending my first formulation against your objection, let me take a quicker way and bring in my second formulation, for this says more than the first one. I believe this second formulation is even more clearly universal, positively as well as negatively: it will serve to determine all positive duties as well as all negative ones. And it will clearly cover cases like priests and soldiers, more easily and clearly than the first formulation.

SOCRATES: To that, then, we must turn next. But before we do, I want to explore one more question regarding your "Golden Rule". We have confined ourselves to the purely logical question of its universality: Is it as wide-ranging, as complete, as you claim? An equally important problem, it seems to me, is its emptiness, the fact that it has no content, that it is merely formal rather than material.

KANT: I do not see that as a problem. It is necessary that if the rule is universal, it must abstract from particular content. So its formality, or "emptiness", follows from its universality. A law of logic says that as you increase the extension, or universality, of any concept, you proportionately decrease its comprehension, or specific content. The more universal a concept is, the more empty and nonspecific it must be. You can't have both.

SOCRATES: Yes, but universals are still full of content even when very general. For example, "human nature" is a universal, and it abstracts from accidental differences like male or female, old or young, but it still contains a rich content. In fact almost the whole of anthropology and psychology is concerned with it. And yet you say in your Preface that your ethics will *not* depend on anthropology or anything else we learn from experience. You say this in *praise* of your system. The very thing your critics most often blame in it—its purely formal and contentless character— is what you praise.

KANT: I do. And that is because this is the only way to avoid disagreement. If it were based on anthropology, some people would agree with it and others would disagree with it, because its conclusions would be relative to its premises, which would be contingent on experience, which is not exactly the same for everyone, and on the interpretation of experience, which is even more diverse.

SOCRATES: I wonder why you assume that this disagreement would be too high a price to pay for an ethics with content. Throughout all of human history, people have never agreed universally about any controversial philosophical point. Is it not a bit arrogant to assume that you would be able to lead them to the Promised Land for the first time?

KANT: The thought is not original with me. Descartes first conceived it, at the beginning of his *Discourse on Method*.

SOCRATES: True. And you might look into the conversation I had with him here about precisely that question.

But I want now to pursue another dimension of this empty a priori formalism of your ethics; and this is what I think is your system's most important limitation, or cutting away, or pruning, compared with all the other systems.

All of them believed in some kind of a natural moral law, except for the Sophists, who are not worthy to be compared with you because they simply had no ethics at all, only ethos; no morals, only mores. All of the other ancient philosophers had some transcendent or absolute goods or rights or oughts that were full of content, like the Ten Commandments.

KANT: Yes, and they never could agree about what the best set of laws was. Or the best goal, the best good. They all claimed to know the *summum bonum*, the "greatest good", and yet ten different philosophers discovered ten different "greatest goods", but the earth can have only one north pole.

SOCRATES: But even though they did not agree about the nature of the greatest good, they all agreed that it existed.

And this natural law, this transcendent dimension, this vertical dimension, so to speak, let them limit our free choices, and distinguish between liberty and license, and discriminate between good and evil. For instance, the Ten Commandments defined ten evils in ten areas of human life. Buddha's "noble eightfold path" did the same with eight goods.

KANT: I do the same with my "categorical imperative", *without* a "natural law". I am a moral absolutist too, but I have only one moral absolute instead of eight or ten.

SOCRATES: I wonder whether you really have moral absolutism there, as you think you do.

KANT: Why do you doubt that?

SOCRATES: Because your one absolute, your "categorical imperative", has no content, as the moral absolutes of other moral absolutists do.

KANT: Why do you think that makes it less than absolute?

SOCRATES: Because when you empty out all the content of the absolute "natural law", the "vertical" law, so to speak, you have to fill in all the content "horizontally", so that the only limitation of the exercise of your will in free choice that you allow is a horizontal one, defined by the relationship between your will and other people's wills. That sounds like relativism rather than absolutism.

KANT: No. The one rule, the "categorical imperative", the "Golden Rule", is an absolute.

SOCRATES: But none of its content is. That content comes not from the natural law but from the relationship between what you will and what other people will: if the relationship is equality, good; if not, bad. For you, the moral limit on free choice comes only from the Golden Rule of equality—do unto others whatever you will they do to you. But equality is a relative notion, not an absolute one. In your ethical system, I am just if I grant to everyone else the same rights I claim for myself, *whatever* those rights may be. That "whatever" makes it sound relative, not absolute.

KANT: It is exactly the opposite. The "whatever", the emptiness of content that you are complaining about, is precisely what makes my imperative universal and therefore absolute.

SOCRATES: And you believe that it is necessary to abandon the old absolutes, full of content, the fullness of the old "natural law"? This is the price you have to pay for keeping your imperative absolute?

KANT: Yes. It is like the law of noncontradiction in logic. All other rules are relative to it, justified by it. And it is supremely formal, or empty of content.

SOCRATES: Why then did previous ethical thinkers not think you had to pay this price? Why did they have universal and absolute imperatives with content?

KANT: Because they rested their ethics on an anthropology.

SOCRATES: They did. That's why they called it the "natural law": it was the law of human nature. And you do not do that because . . . ?

KANT: Because I seek the most certain ethical principle of all. People disagreed about anthropology, and therefore also about ethics, insofar as their ethics was based on their anthropology. In freeing my ethics from anthropology I free it from disagreement and uncertainty.

SOCRATES: So it is Descartes' demand for certainty that drives you.

KANT: In a way that it did not drive premodern philosophers, yes. Once Descartes' "critical problem" is raised, whether in epistemology or in ethics, it cannot be ignored. We cannot simply return to premodern naïveté. So you cannot fairly compare me with premodern philosophers like Plato or Aristotle or Aquinas.

SOCRATES: Let me compare you with two modern philosophers then, one before you and one after you, on this issue that we are discussing, namely, the emptiness of content of your moral absolute and the consequent need to fill in the content not absolutely, or "vertically", by the natural law, but horizontally, or relatively, by the relationship of equality between you and others, between your will and their will.

One of these philosophers came before you: Rousseau. He too was a moralist, and he too had no "vertical" natural law, but only the "horizontal" limit on free choice provided by "the general will", which he said was infallible as long as it was free. You seem to say the same, thus ascribing the divine attribute (infallibility) to the human will while denying it, or at least ignoring it, in the divine will.

KANT: My ethics is a humanistic ethics, not a theistic ethics. That is the only way I can expect to secure universal agreement, for everyone believes in the human, but not everyone believes in the divine.

SOCRATES: I wonder why you demand or expect universal agreement. No one did before Descartes.

KANT: No one thought it was possible before Descartes, or rather before modernity, and the discovery of the scientific method—the only method that has ever persuaded all men to universally agreed conclusions.

SOCRATES: So you really are a child of Descartes, then, and your ethics is really the fulfillment of the task he did not live long enough to perform: the application of the scientific method to philosophy, even to ethics.

KANT: In a sense. I do not accept his rationalism in epistemology, which I called "dogmatic", but I accept his new hope of finding universal agreement through something like the scientific method.

SOCRATES: Do you not find it ironic to be in agreement with Rousseau, of all people, on the point we are discussing—the point that the moral absolute, the "vertical" law, is contentless and gets content only from the relationship between human wills? Rousseau, after all, was a great enemy of the idea that science had provided the key to progress in ethics. He also was the champion of sentiment against reason. He seems a strange bedfellow for you.

KANT: Surely one can agree with another philosopher on one point without agreeing on all the others. Who is the second philosopher you want to compare me to?

SOCRATES: His name is John Stuart Mill, and you did not know him because he lived after you. He is often called the father of utilitarianism, which is the exact opposite of your ethics. It is relativistic; it says, in effect, that the end justifies the means, and its standard for judging all behavior is that an act is good in proportion to its likelihood to have good consequences, which Mill defined as "the greatest happiness of the greatest number". Every step in that argument you have taken pains to reject, as if you saw it looming on the horizon, like a prophet. And yet you agree with his denial of an absolute, or "vertical", natural moral law.

KANT: You apparently know the future, Socrates. Can you tell me whether my philosophy will take root in the world in the generations after mine? Or will the battle be won by these two forms of moral relativism that you mentioned—Rousseau's sentimentalism and Mill's utilitarianism—or perhaps by some other forms of relativism?

SOCRATES: I can tell you that these two philosophies that you reject—sentimentalism and utilitarianism— will come together and take root in America, which will become the most powerful nation in the world. And I can tell you that the preference for equality rather than excellence, which is at the heart of both of these philosophies, will come to define the American character. It's all in a book called *Democracy in America* by a Frenchman named Alexis de Tocqueville. You will be allowed to read it here. In this place you can get at the books of the future as well as the books of the past.

KANT: I look forward with great relish to reading them. As for your criticism of my contentless ethics,

Socrates, I think you will find the content you seek if you look at the second formulation of my "categorical imperative".

SOCRATES: Then we will do just that.

15

The Second Formulation of the Categorical Imperative: Personalism

SOCRATES: Your second formulation of the "categorical imperative" is indeed much more positive and full of content than the first. So much, in fact, that it would seem to be not just another formulation but another imperative. You begin by saying: **"Now I** G 428 **say that man, and in general every rational being, exists as an end in himself and not merely as a means to be arbitrarily used by this or that will."**

I noticed immediately that you begin with an "is" statement, a statement of what is—a statement of metaphysics, in fact.

KANT: Yes. It is a synthetic a priori.

SOCRATES: But I thought you claimed to prove that metaphysics was impossible in your *Critique of Pure Reason*.

KANT: Impossible for theoretical reason, yes, but not for practical reason. I believe this is where metaphysics can be salvaged—here, in the area of practical reason.

SOCRATES: After it has proved necessary to abandon it earlier, in theoretical reason.

KANT: Yes.

SOCRATES: That would seem to be very surprising, to put it mildly: something like a sea captain abandoning a sinking ship and then finding that same ship afloat in another sea.

KANT: You cannot argue from analogies, Socrates.

SOCRATES: I know. I am not arguing yet, just reconnoitering.
   Your next step is to immediately deduce from this "is" statement an "ought" statement, or a "must" statement: **"He must in all his actions, whether** Ibid. **directed to himself or to other rational beings, always be regarded at the same time as an end."**

KANT: Yes. I do not regard such a deduction as fallacious, as some philosophers do. I do not totally divorce the "ought" from the "is".

SOCRATES: Oh, neither do I. But you realize, of course, that in order for your argument to be valid you must be assuming another premise. You argue that

1. Every rational being is an end and not a means. ·

2. Therefore every rational being should be treated as an end and not as a means.

Do you see what this logically assumes?

KANT: Of course. That everything should be treated as what it is.

SOCRATES: Yes indeed. And I would call this the "three Rs principle," or the Right Response to Reality principle.

KANT: So what is the problem?

SOCRATES: To admit the "three Rs principle" is to admit that ethics must be based on metaphysics, is it not? That what is *right* must be based on what *is*. This is what you do here, when you go beyond your first formulation of the categorical imperative, is it not?

KANT: Yes and no. The second formulation does supply metaphysical content in distinguishing persons from things. But it "works" in exactly the same way as the first formulation: by formal logical consistency, by a kind of law of equality. We are to treat ourselves and others equally, that is, as equally absolute ends and not merely as relative means. And this is what the Jewish and Christian Scriptures also imply when they tell us to love our neighbors *as ourselves*. I merely "unpack" that morality. It is a morality of equality. It is like a reversible equation: if we are to love our neighbors as we love ourselves, we are also to love ourselves as we love our neighbors.

SOCRATES: That is certainly admirably logical, and I don't think many would dispute that principle. But it does not seem to be the morality of the Scriptures, as you claim it is. For the morality we find there has a vertical dimension too, a dimension of excellence, as well as a horizontal dimension of equality.

KANT: I did indeed separate those two dimensions and appealed only to what you call the dimension of equality, the horizontal one, the human one. For that is based on universal human reason, and we can expect all rational and moral men to agree with it. The other dimension is based on faith and divine revelation, and we can expect the world to disagree endlessly about it. There are many religions, and many scriptures, and many different "vertical" moralities in the world. I do not see how they can agree. But if we do not separate the human and rational dimension of the ethics of our scriptures from the religious dimension, I do not see how we can win a universal hearing for it.

SOCRATES: I understand your strategy now. You are probably right. And yet, to separate those two dimensions as you do seems like removing the soul from the body. What you have left when you do that is a ghost or a corpse. And certainly, the ethics in the scriptures do seem to be something like a single living body with a soul, rather than something like a two-layer cake or a two-story building that you can separate nicely into its two parts and keep the one unchanged even while you abandon the other.

KANT: I would dispute that.

SOCRATES: Would you dispute Jesus' teachings in the famous "Sermon on the Mount"?

KANT: Certainly not.

SOCRATES: Would you agree that that is the central summary of his morality?

KANT: I would indeed.

SOCRATES: But all his imperatives for this world are connected with, and based on, some truth about the next. Each of the Beatitudes, which are the sum and summit of the whole sermon, is justified by something about Heaven, or the Kingdom of Heaven.

KANT: Are we here to discuss the New Testament or the *Grounding for the Metaphysics of Morals?*

SOCRATES: Touché. I accept your programmatic correction and return to your text.

Next, you go on to explain the connection between ethics and psychology, or anthropology. That is another subject that, like metaphysics, I thought you had abandoned. Didn't you say that in your Preface?

KANT: I here explain a *connection* between ethics and psychology, or anthropology; but that does not mean that I *derive* ethics from psychology or anthropology. The connection is simply that objects of psychological inclinations, or personal needs and desires, have only a conditioned ethical value and thus are subject to only hypothetical imperatives, for these inclinations are directed toward "things" rather than persons. In contrast, objects of moral duty have intrinsic value and thus are subject to a categorical imperative because the moral will under duty is directed toward persons:

G 428   **All the objects of inclinations have only a conditioned value; for if there were not these inclinations and the needs founded on them, then their object would be without value. . . . The value of any object attainable by our action is always conditioned. Beings whose**

existence depends ... on nature have ...
if they are not rational beings, only a relative value as means and are therefore called
things. On the other hand, rational beings
are called persons inasmuch as their nature
already marks them out as ends in themselves, i.e., as something which is not to be
used merely as means, and ... which are
thus objects of respect. Persons are, therefore, not merely subjective ends, whose existence ... has a value for us, but such beings are objective ends, i.e., exist as ends in
themselves. ...

The practical imperative will therefore be   G 429
the following: Act in such a way that you
treat humanity, whether in your own person or in the person of another, always at
the same time as an end and never simply as
a means.

That is the heart of my second formulation of the
categorical imperative and its justification; and, really, that is the heart of my ethics.

SOCRATES: So you set side by side and contrast the
following opposites:

1.	Non-rational beings in nature	Rational beings, persons
2.	Objects of inclination	Objects of moral duty (implied)
3.	Objects of conditioned or relative value	Objects of unconditioned or absolute value
4.	Subjective ends, of value only for us	Objective ends, of value in themselves

| 5. | Means in themselves | Ends in themselves |
| 6. | To be used merely as means | To be respected as ends, not merely used as means |

Is that correct?

KANT: Yes. And admirably clear.

SOCRATES: Well, this certainly looks like metaphysics to me. For you say it is the *nature* of persons that justifies our treating them as ends in themselves—a very metaphysical statement indeed. Our moral duty is to treat persons as ends *because they are* ends. That presupposes the "three Rs principle."

KANT: I do not deny your "three Rs principle", Socrates. It is self-evident.

SOCRATES: But it is metaphysics! The first of these six sets of opposites is the metaphysics of persons, what persons really are as distinct from what nonrational beings in nature really are.

And the second one is psychology, or anthropology. It relates two different kinds of objective *beings* to two different kinds of human subjective response to them. It says that nonrational objects are objects of inclination, or desire, but that persons are not. I assume this means, or implies, that they are the objects of duty, and thus of the moral will.

KANT: Yes, that is what I mean.

SOCRATES: And then the third and fourth contrasts relate metaphysics to value theory, or what will be called axiology. They distinguish things of subjective value from things of objective value, and things of relative value from things of absolute value. These are not quite the same distinction, are they: the subjective versus the objective and the relative versus the absolute?

KANT: No, but they are connected, and they overlap here. Shall I prove that to you?

SOCRATES: No, that seems pretty obvious. And then your fifth contrast is the traditional distinction between means and ends. But you take pains to say that the things in the first column, which you call "means", are not merely whatever happens to be *sought* as means or *treated* as means or *desired* as means by any persons, but those things which *are* means *in themselves*, while the things in column two are things that really *are* ends *in themselves*. Again, this is metaphysics, and clearly labeled as such: things-in-themselves!

KANT: Well, yes. This is how we have access to things-in-themselves: not with theoretical reason but with practical reason.

SOCRATES: And the sixth contrast, which is purely ethical, depends on the other five, especially the one just before it, the fifth. Because of what nonpersons really *are*, namely, only means, they are to be treated as means, and used, while persons, because of what they *are*, because they *are* ends, are to be treated as ends: the three Rs principle.

KANT: Do you blame me for doing metaphysics?

SOCRATES: No, I praise you. I congratulate you on forgetting all about your "Copernican revolution in philosophy" and returning to pre-Kantian metaphysics when you do ethics.

KANT: You are being ironic, Socrates. You are damning me with faint praise. I knew it would come to this, even when we got to that part of my philosophy which you praise the most. You just have to tear every philosophy apart somehow, don't you?

SOCRATES: But I have no desire to tear your ethics apart, certainly not this second formulation of the categorical imperative. That would be something akin to a blasphemy. For these ideas appear to me as something more than merely correct; they appear to me as something holy.

KANT: Oh. I am surprised to hear you say that, Socrates.

SOCRATES: Why? Did you think I had no capacity for detecting holy things?

KANT: No. Clearly, in the "Euthyphro" dialogue, you knew what holiness was, though you claimed not to know, and Euthyphro did not, though he claimed to know it.

In fact, I had long suspected and hoped that your penchant for logical disputation was not the deepest thing in you. Your most personally revealing speeches, in the *Apology* and the *Symposium*, give us instead the picture of a kind of agnostic saint.

SOCRATES: I was far from being a saint.

KANT: But you were not far from being a *seeker* of sanctity.

SOCRATES: That is true.

KANT: Some suspicious scholars tell us that that dimension in you was largely the invention of Plato, that he admired you so uncritically that he virtually made you into a god. But this is not so, is it? Can I safely assume that the Socrates of Plato's dialogues and the Socrates who stands before me now are the same person?

SOCRATES: Yes. If the Socrates of Plato's dialogues had been his invention and not the real me, Plato would have been laughed out of Athens when he published them. Most Athenians—both my friends and my enemies—still remembered me vividly when Plato published. So he didn't dare go far off the tracks of real history.

But we are not here to talk about me, but about you.

You asked, a moment ago, how well your ethics fared after your death. I will tell you this much: there is no passage penned by any modern philosopher on the subject of ethics that is more admired and accepted by more people, both philosophers and nonphilosophers, and by people of all religions and none, than this one.

KANT: I am humbled.

SOCRATES: You are a humble man, Immanuel, unlike most philosophers I have met. But I do have some questions about this.

KANT: I thought so. I fear I will now be not just humbled but humiliated.

SOCRATES: Not at all. That is not the purpose of my questioning, as you well know.

I only want to see the truth more clearly; that is why I scrub everyone's mental windows so vigorously.

KANT: But you want to tear my philosophy into two parts, the epistemology and the ethics, which you say are contradictory.

SOCRATES: Well, you *did* say we simply could not know things as they are in themselves back in your *Critique of Pure Reason,* and now you make the heart of your ethics dependent on a statement about what persons and things really are in themselves. That does seem contradictory. Can you show me how it isn't?

KANT: I think so. As you know, to overcome an apparent contradiction, we must make a distinction. And I distinguish theoretical reason and practical reason.

SOCRATES: And by practical reason you mean the rational will, the will of a rational creature?

KANT: Yes.

SOCRATES: So what we cannot *know* theoretically, we can still *will* practically?

KANT: Yes.

SOCRATES: How can we will a thing if we do not know what it is?

KANT: We *do* know it, in a way. It is *rational* will, not a blind force. We can *conceive* it, but we cannot *prove* it exists.

SOCRATES: But you do base your imperative on what really exists, namely, persons, and on what we know persons really are, namely, ends.

KANT: Yes. But we cannot *prove* this. We can only *postulate*, on the basis of moral necessity, what we cannot prove on the basis of logical necessity.

SOCRATES: But we must assume that we can *know* the difference between persons and things. You do not say that we *willed* this distinction into existence, do you?

KANT: No.

SOCRATES: I think we ought to take the time out to define and distinguish a few different acts of the human soul: first, what are traditionally called the three acts of the mind, namely, conceiving, judging, and proving, and then also, in the second place, willing, and in the third place, postulating, which seems to be an act of both mind and will.

KANT: I do not contrast mind and will as sharply as you do, Socrates. What I mean by "will" *is* practical reason, and thus a form of knowing. I do not limit reason to theoretical reason, and I do not limit will to some blind force of desire. "Reason" *includes* will.

SOCRATES: So you have a *broader* conception of "reason" than the traditional one. I thought you had a *narrower* one, since you meant by "reason" only "proving", not "conceiving" or understanding, which the ancients included under "reason"—all three "acts of the mind", but only the mind, and not the will.

I think this question about defining reason and will needs a much longer exploration. But however important that tangent is, it would take us a long time now to do justice to it. So I think we should postpone it until another time and return to your text.

I would like to know where you got this noble idea, this second formulation of your categorical imperative.

KANT: Do you mean what were my historical sources?

SOCRATES: That was not what I meant, but I am curious about that too.

KANT: First of all, the most obvious one.

SOCRATES: What is that?

KANT: The Gospels, of course.

SOCRATES: Oh. Now it is my turn to be a bit humbled. But what I meant by asking what your sources were, was not your *historical* sources but your *logical* sources. What was the logical derivation of this second formulation of the "categorical imperative"? You led up to your first formulation step by step, through preliminary steps. But the second does not seem to logically follow from the first. It seems to drop like a bolt from the sky.

KANT: I do not say that we can deduce it logically from the first formulation alone. It clearly says more than the first formulation does. But it says that "more" *within* the first formulation, not outside it. It unpacks the first one. In the terms of my first *Critique*, it is "transcendental": it gives us the conditions of possibility for the first to be true. It *explains why* the first is true. It is not an argument but an explanation.

And it functions, or "works", in exactly the same way as the first one does: it is a universal criterion of all moral duties. That is why I do not call it a second imperative but a second formulation of the one and only categorical imperative.

SOCRATES: But your second formulation does seem to go beyond the first in its functioning because it seems to be a universal *positive* criterion as well as a universal negative one, which is all that the first formulation was, if our analysis was correct.

KANT: No, I claim that both formulations have the same universality.

SOCRATES: Hmmm . . . perhaps you are right. For on second thought, your second formulation may not be universal either.

KANT: Why not?

SOCRATES: Because it does not seem to cover *all* moral duties. In terms of the Ten Commandments, it does not seem to cover the first table of the law, only the second. I do not see how either your first or second formulation condemns idolatry, disobedience to the first commandment. And that is the first and greatest commandment, according to the man you say you take as your moral model and master. It is the first and greatest commandment for Muslims and Jews too, as well as for Christians.

So an atheist, a polytheist, or an idolater could be perfectly moral without disobeying either your first or second formulations.

KANT: Well of course he could. That's what makes it universal. That's a plus, not a minus, for my ethics.

SOCRATES: Only if atheism is true.

KANT: Why do you say that?

SOCRATES: Because if God in fact exists, then it is surely unjust not to include Him under the three R rule, isn't it? Is it not an injustice to God to refuse to acknowledge Him as what He is? Is this not at least as great an injustice as not to acknowledge your earthly father?

KANT: But my ethics does not mean to extend to such things as religion.

SOCRATES: Why not? Are there not duties there too?

KANT: But we cannot *know* what our duties are there because we cannot know whether God exists or not. We can only believe. My ethics is based on knowledge by reason, not on religious belief. You should appreciate that: you were an agnostic.

SOCRATES: But even if you cannot know whether God exists or not, if there is even a chance that He does exist, would you not still have a duty to acknowledge Him for fear of doing Him an injustice?

KANT: You cannot do an injustice to someone who does not exist. And the agnostic does not claim to know that God exists and usually claims that no one can know.

SOCRATES: But he also does not know that God does *not* exist. Take a parallel case. Suppose there is a chance that a certain court jester is really the king in disguise. Would it not be right to treat him with the respect due to the king rather than with the scorn due to the jester? So do you not have a duty to consider that possibility, to ensure against injustice?

Or suppose you are out hunting with your friend, and you see a sudden movement in the bushes. The movement may well be a deer, but is also may be your friend. If you do not know which it is, do you not have a moral responsibility to act as if it is your friend and refrain from shooting, to ensure against the injustice of killing an innocent man?

KANT: Of course. But I think these cases are a little bit different. . . .

SOCRATES: Then let's take still another one, to be clear about the common principle I am trying to establish. Suppose you have been given a gift of a large sum of money by an anonymous donor. Many people say that the donor is a mysterious Mister X who writes letters to you but whom you have never seen. In fact, you do not even know whether he is real; he may be a fiction invented by a Mister Y. Would you not have a moral obligation to write your thanks to Mister X just in case he is real and he was the giver of the money?

KANT: Mister X is an allegory for God, is he not?

SOCRATES: Yes.

KANT: And you are complaining that I keep God out of my ethics.

SOCRATES: Yes.

KANT: But I do bring God in. But I bring Him in at the end rather than at the beginning. I appeal to agnostics as well as theists by not starting with God, and by saying that we should all act as if there were a righteous God even though we cannot know whether there is or not. So I agree with your Mister X example.

SOCRATES: Then why not include the first table of the Mosaic law in your ethics as well as the second? Why not worship and pray to the God Who may well exist, to avoid injustice?

KANT: I do not at all disagree with that argument, Socrates! I wanted to free ethics, not from all religious duties, but from religious dogmatism.

SOCRATES: Do you agree, then, that there are three kinds of moral obligations, or three moral questions, or three aspects of human life that ethics must deal with, and not only one . . . ?

KANT: You mean the three traditional moral determinants, the act itself and the motive and the circumstances? I know you fault me for making morality dependent only on motive, not on the nature of the act itself or the circumstances. You made that point before. But my reason is . . .

SOCRATES: No, this is *another*, different case of your getting "only one out of three". Ethics has traditionally addressed the three questions that any team, any army, any fleet of ships, any cooperating group, must ask. How to cooperate, how to treat each other, is only one of these three questions. A second one is how each individual is to stay healthy or shipshape or virtuous. In ethics that is the question of character, of virtues and vices, of good or bad moral habits. And this question you totally eliminate. And you also ignore the third question, and the most important of all, which is what the mission of the group is and how to accomplish it—in other words, the end, the *summum bonum*. And that is a question that every religion claims to answer, though by a different method: faith rather than reason. So you seem to ignore the two most important questions of ethics.

KANT: But these are metaphysical questions, Socrates, the third one especially.

SOCRATES: But in your second formulation of the categorical imperative, I thought you finally did get back into metaphysics. You said each person *is* an end. I guess you only got your feet a little wet and then backed off.

KANT: I have already given my reasons for rejecting transcendent metaphysics. We will get nowhere by going over all that again.

SOCRATES: How do you know we won't?

KANT: I suppose I don't, and I suppose we might; but can't we just get on with your critique of my ethics instead of returning to the question of metaphysics?

SOCRATES: You are right. For our readers' patience is not infinite. Back to your text.

There is another reason I prefer your second formulation of the categorical imperative to the first: it seems more adequate than the first in that it discovers and labels the more ultimate object of moral loyalty, namely, *the person, not the law.*

KANT: Both are ultimate objects, Socrates. Both are absolutes.

SOCRATES: But one absolute can still be subordinate to another, can't it?

KANT: How?

SOCRATES: As one infinity is less than another.

KANT: How can one infinity be less than another?

SOCRATES: The sum of all positive integers is infinite, is it not?

KANT: Potentially infinite, yes.

SOCRATES: And the sum of all odd-numbered positive integers is also infinite.

KANT: Yes.

SOCRATES: But odd numbers are only half of all numbers. So this one infinity is only half as large as the other.

KANT: I admit that principle. How do you apply it now to my two formulations? Do you mean that my first formulation covers only negative duties and not positive ones so it is like the infinity of only odd numbered positive integers?

SOCRATES: I mean that too. But I meant mainly this: that even though both imperatives are absolutes, I think your first formulation is ethically relative to the second.

KANT: Why?

SOCRATES: It's moral common sense, isn't it? If my wife asked me why I was faithful to her, do you think she would be pleased if I answered: "Only because I wanted to obey the moral law"?

KANT: No.

SOCRATES: Why? Because the primary object of my faithfulness should be *her*. I am faithful to her, not to the law, first of all. The law was not the *object* but the *definition* of my faithfulness. And so on in all other cases.

KANT: I will admit this. The second formulation is superior to the first, and more absolute. However, I maintain that both formulations give the same judgment on all cases.

SOCRATES: Let's see. Let's consider a specific case to see whether your two imperatives would function in the same way and label the same acts morally right or wrong.

In most areas of human life, such as lying, cheating, stealing, killing, honoring parents, doing justice, giving mercy and generosity, and facing danger, it seems you are right. Injustice, cruelty, stinginess, theft, murder, and lying all sin against both the Golden Rule and against the other person.

But there is one area where it seems your second formula would seem to exclude more acts than the first.

KANT: Where?

SOCRATES: Sexual behavior.

KANT: Why do you single that out?

SOCRATES: Because if someone wanted to believe in
the rest of traditional morality but not traditional
sexual morality, they could use your first formulation to justify any sexual activity that did not cause
immediate personal harm or unhappiness to the other
person. Thus every sexual act would be justified as
long as the actor willed that everyone do it: lust, mas-
turbation, fornication, consenting adultery, sodomy,
orgies, bestiality, almost anything, as long as all those
involved were freely consenting adults in possession
of their intellectual sanity.

But your second formulation would be more demanding of respect for the other's sexuality, and not
just the other's will. Is this not so?

KANT: No.

SOCRATES: Why not?

KANT: I maintain that the first formulation of the imperative is still universal. It would cover traditional
sexual morality too. This "world of orgies" might be
willed by foolish young unmarried men but certainly
not by married men in possession of their sanity, or,
certainly, by women.

Why do you look surprised, Socrates?

SOCRATES: I am surprised at how much wisdom about
women is now coming from the mouth of a lifelong
bachelor.

Let's look at this "world of orgies" from the viewpoint of each of your two formulations.

It seems very clear, at any rate, that "a world of
orgies" could not be willed if we obeyed the second
formulation of the "categorical imperative". For the

"respect" it demands toward all persons is almost the exact opposite of lust. "Respect" of the other person as an *end* in himself is clearly not compatible with *using* the other person as a *means* to one's own advantage or pleasure, whether the pleasure is sexual or any other kind. And this is what lust essentially means, whether it is only in fantasy or in action.

So even if it is mutually consensual and free, and even if it produces effects of happiness in all parties concerned, lust is still selfish rather than unselfish.

And it certainly flows from inclination and not duty.

So it would be condemned by your second formulation.

But all this seems to say far more than the first formulation does. It gives the reason for traditional sexual morality. The first formulation does not. It would seem to allow for anything freely and mutually consented to, including sadomasochism or double-gendered prostitution.

KANT: No, I think the first formulation too would condemn lust.

SOCRATES: I do not see why. Certainly some people— those foolish young unmarried men—could still consistently will everyone to participate in their "world of orgies".

KANT: I think a "world of orgies" is a little extreme and fanciful, don't you? Only a thoughtless barbarian would really will that. The price to pay would be too high.

SOCRATES: What price?

KANT: Fathering illegitimate children.

SOCRATES: But suppose that price was not required. Suppose there were a simple, safe, reliable, and cheap contraceptive available to any and all.

KANT: There would still be social stigmas and shame.

SOCRATES: Suppose a new psychology "contracepted" *that*?

KANT: That would be a "brave new world" indeed.

SOCRATES: After this conversation, I am going to let you read a prophetic novel with that title written in the twentieth century. I think you will be very surprised.

16

The Third Formulation of the Categorical Imperative: The Autonomy of the Will

SOCRATES: You have one more formulation of the "categorical imperative". Here it is: **"The . . . third formulation of the principle . . . [is] the idea of the will of every rational being as a will that legislates universal law. . . . Autonomy of the will is the property that the will has of being a law to itself."** See G 432 G 440

So you identify three things here: the *autonomy* of the will, the will being a law unto itself, and the will as *legislating* universal law. Is that right? Are these essentially three different ways of saying the same thing?

KANT: Yes.

SOCRATES: And you call this **"the . . . third formulation of the principle".** By **"the principle"** do you mean the categorical imperative?

KANT: Yes.

SOCRATES: I do not see how this is another formulation of the same categorical imperative.

First of all, I do not see how it is an imperative at all. You do not formulate it as a law to be obeyed but as a truth to be discovered.

KANT: It is a transcendental deduction of the preconditions of possibility for experience: for the moral experience of obligation that I have already formulated in my first two formulations of the categorical imperative.

SOCRATES: I understand that. But it is not an imperative.

KANT: No, but it is *about* moral imperatives. It is the principle that distinguishes authentic moral imperatives from inauthentic moral imperatives. And here is the principle:

> **Autonomy of the will [is] the supreme principle of morality . . .**
>
> **Heteronomy of the will [is] the source of all spurious principles of morality . . .**
>
> **If the will . . . goes outside of itself and seeks this law in the character of any of its objects, then heteronomy always results. The will in that case does not give itself the law, but the object does so because of its relation to the will. This relation, whether it rests on inclination or on representations of reason, admits only of hypothetical imperatives: I ought to do something because I will something else.**

G 441

So you see, this is an ethical or moral principle. The ultimate one, in fact.

SOCRATES: But it is not an ethics that tells us what we should do or not do, as the first two formulations do. It is really meta-ethics rather than ethics: an ethics that discriminates between good and bad ethical systems rather than between good and bad acts.

KANT: That is correct. It is what you call meta-ethics. We are arguing only about labels.

SOCRATES: All right, then. In your meta-ethics, you say the will is a law unto itself. Surely you do not mean by that that whatever I will to do becomes morally good for me from the mere fact that I will it, do you? Because if you do, then by definition nothing can be evil.

KANT: No, of course not. That would be a self-contradiction: a moral law that distinguished good from evil by not labeling anything evil, thus by *not* distinguishing good from evil.

Let me try to explain my point in traditional terms you are more familiar with. I am not speaking here of the "*formal* cause", or definition, of good and evil. The first two formulations give us that. I am speaking here of the "*efficient* cause" of the moral law—that very moral law that formally discriminates between good and evil. My question here is not: What does the law command us to do now? But: Where did this law come from in the first place?

SOCRATES: I see. Do you think the practical reason (the will) is related to the moral law as the theoretical reason (the mind) is related to the laws of thought?

KANT: In most ways, yes. Why do you ask?

SOCRATES: Because if it is, then your third formulation must be untrue. For surely the mind of man is not the author of the law of noncontradiction, is it?

KANT: Not in the sense that *I* invented it . . .

SOCRATES: So why must the will of man be the author of the moral law? In other words, if the mind is heteronymous, and *under* authority (the authority of logical laws), rather than *over* that authority, or the *cause* of that authority, why is not the will also heteronymous, and under moral authority rather than the cause of it? Why are not these two parallel?

KANT: They *are* parallel, but they are both autonomous. That was precisely the point of my "Copernican revolution in philosophy". And the autonomy of the will is the perfect parallel to it in ethics. Just as the mind makes intellectual forms, the will makes moral laws.

SOCRATES: Do you mean that the human mind is the author of the law of noncontradiction and the sole authority for that law? You admitted a moment ago that we did not invent the law of noncontradiction.

KANT: Not by our immediately-known ego, which I call the "empirical ego". This active authorship is the work of the transcendental ego, both in mind and will, theoretical and practical reason, epistemology and ethics.

And I say that the mind is the author only of form and structure and meaning, but not of the *truth* of judgments. The law of noncontradiction was not one of my twelve "categories". Similarly, the will is the author of the moral law, but not of its *rightness*. The categorical imperative is like the law of noncontradiction: its truth is intrinsic to it, not created by our mind or our will or any mind or any will, even the will of God or the gods.

SOCRATES: Not even the will of God? That is significantly different from the will of the gods, you know.

KANT: Not even the will of God. And I thought you would agree with me there, Socrates. For you yourself logically refuted the "divine will theory" of morality in the "Euthyphro".

SOCRATES: But I did not deny that God or the gods willed the good. I only denied that a thing was good only because they willed it. I argued that they willed it because it is good in itself, and God or the gods know that. In other words, for Euthyphro the gods were irrational. Their will did not follow their reason. For me, the gods, if there are true gods, are rational. Their will follows their reason. And all the more must this hold if there is only one perfect God.

KANT: And I agree with you there, Socrates: God is rational. And so are we. That is precisely why our will is autonomous: because it is rational. We can be authors of the moral law, and morality is autonomous, not heteronymous, because it is intrinsically rational, like the law of noncontradiction. If it were heteronymous, as it was for Euthyphro, then it would not be rational and it would not be intrinsic. It would be extrinsic and irrational; it would be another will compelling ours by force or fear. So we agree.

SOCRATES: I wonder whether we do agree.

KANT: Why not?

SOCRATES: You disagree with Euthyphro because his candidate for the author of moral law is irrational, isn't that right?

KANT: Yes.

SOCRATES: And that is the will of the gods.

KANT: Yes.

SOCRATES: And these gods of Euthyphro, and of ancient Greece, are no more or less rational than we humans. They are only more powerful and clever, and immortal.

KANT: Correct.

SOCRATES: So if the gods are just about as rational and as irrational as we are, then we are just about as rational and as irrational as the gods.

KANT: Yes.

SOCRATES: So we are no better or worse candidates for the authorship of the moral law than the gods are.

KANT: Right.

SOCRATES: Now if we substitute the one God for the gods, do you say that the same is true?

KANT: "The same" about what, exactly?

SOCRATES: Euthyphro said that a thing is good because the gods willed it. I said that if there are gods and if they are good and worth obeying, these gods must will a thing because it is good. Now if we substitute "God" for "the gods", there seem to be the same two possibilities: either a thing is good because

God wills it, or God wills it because it is good. Now
if Euthyphro were a monotheist, he would say that a
thing is good only because God willed it. And you and
I would both disagree with that, I think. We would
say that God wills it because it is good, good in itself,
intrinsically good. At least I would say that. Would
you agree with me there?

KANT: Yes. You see, we do agree, Socrates.

SOCRATES: Perhaps. Perhaps not. Let's probe a bit
deeper to find out just how far we do agree.

There are two questions here, not just one. One
is about the role of God versus the role of man in
authoring the moral law. The other is about the role
of reason versus the role of will. My concern now is
the second question.

My problem is that your candidate for the author
of the moral law seems as irrational as Euthyphro's.
The only difference is that it is the human will rather
than the divine will. But it is the will. You see, my
dispute with you is not merely about whether it is the
human will or the divine will that authors the moral
law, but about whether it is will or reason.

KANT: But when I say it is the will I mean the *rational*
will. Will is practical *reason*.

SOCRATES: Then it can be the rational will for God
as well.

KANT: I do not deny that.

SOCRATES: Then why do you say that if morality is
heteronymous and comes from God's will rather than
man's will, that would make it more irrational than

if it is autonomous and comes from the human will?
Is man more rational than God?

KANT: My question in the *Grounding* is not the question of the ultimate origin of the moral law, but of
the immediate origin of it, the origin of it that most
immediately touches the will of man and causes obligation in him. I do not deny that God may be in
fact the *ultimate* author of morality, if He indeed designed man and created man in His own image, with
moral conscience and will—though I say this cannot
be proved and is sheerly a matter of faith.

SOCRATES: But you do believe it? Do you believe it
is true?

KANT: I do.

SOCRATES: And do you believe that no one truth can
ever contradict another truth? That truth, by definition, contradicts only falsehood, not other truth?

KANT: Of course.

SOCRATES: Therefore you believe that there cannot
be any contradiction between any truth that you believe by your religious faith and any truth in the rest
of your philosophy?

KANT: Right. But my faith is not provable by reason.
That's why we call it "faith".

SOCRATES: I understand. So if we find a contradiction
between your rational philosophy and your religious
faith, then either your philosophy or your faith must
be false.

KANT: That logically follows. Where do you see such a contradiction?

SOCRATES: I do not see it until I look. But I want to look.

KANT: Where?

SOCRATES: In two places: in your idea of the role of God and in your idea of the role of man, the role of human will and conscience.

KANT: What problem do you see in my idea of the role of God?

SOCRATES: For you, God seems to be no longer the sovereign. Man is. Man replaces God as the author of the moral law.

KANT: The immediate author, yes. Perhaps not the ultimate author—though that is a matter of faith, not proof.

SOCRATES: Do you see what follows from this?

KANT: What?

SOCRATES: That man rather than God is the *judge*.

KANT: Why must that follow?

SOCRATES: Because the one who authors the law is the one who has the right to judge by the law, is that not so?

KANT: That is so.

SOCRATES: And therefore man becomes the judge as well as the author.

KANT: I agree with that conclusion.

SOCRATES: Then what role is left for God in this system? If it is not the role of either author or judge, whatever is left seems like a bone thrown to a dog.

KANT: I realize that pious readers will at first be shocked when they meet this idea, that man rather than God is the immediate author of moral law— and that therefore when we die and come to the Last Judgment, we will find ourselves rather than God sitting on the throne judging us. But I say this *must* be true, because only then will we be silenced; only then will we be unable to argue with the Judge, for the Judge will not be an other but the self.

And even if He *were* an other, He cannot be a mere other, but *we* must agree with His judgment by our conscience. Otherwise, it would be simply a question of power and might rather than right. There must be an identity between God's concept of "right" and our concept of "right" if the judgment is to be a moral judgment, a judgment by right, rather than simply a matter of power. God is of course the superior power, but God having superior power does not give God superior right. Might does not make right for God any more than for man.

In morality, right makes might; might does not make right. And the might that right makes is purely moral might, the power to bind the conscience, not the body or the feelings and fears, including the fear of punishment.

SOCRATES: I agree with your moral principle there. That was one of the few things I claimed to know was true, and I tried to defend this point against Thrasymachus in Book 1 of Plato's *Republic*. It is true, as you say, that God's superiority in power does not give Him any moral authority over us. But if God is God, must not God be also superior in right, as well as in might? Must not God be morally perfect?

KANT: Yes indeed.

SOCRATES: And would not that give Him moral authority over man, if authority depends on right rather than on might? For even a good *man* has a moral authority over an evil man by reason of his righteousness. An unrighteous and corrupt man has no right to judge a righteous and innocent man, but a righteous man does have the right to judge an unrighteous man. How much more would the all-righteous God have the moral authority to judge us?

KANT: I do not deny that God has authority over man. But it is not an immediate authority. The immediate authority is the intrinsic rightness of the moral law. God wills it, but He wills it because it is good; it is not good because He wills it—as you yourself proved against Euthyphro. So it is the intrinsic rightness and goodness of morality that is the supreme authority, not God. That's why it must be man's conscience, not God, that is the immediate judge of morality.

SOCRATES: I do not deny that moral goodness is intrinsic, not extrinsic. That is precisely the position of the old "natural law" moralists. And I do not deny that God may well have delegated His own authority to His prophet in the rational soul of man, the prophet we call conscience. I do not deny that it is not God but His prophet in the soul that directly addresses man. But suppose that prophet speaks with absolute authority *because* he speaks in the name of God.

KANT: But if so, then God cannot be not extrinsic to that prophet, the moral conscience, the rational will. That is why morality is autonomous, not heteronymous.

SOCRATES: When you say "not extrinsic", so you mean that God is simply moral conscience itself? That God is not an Other? Are you a pantheist?

KANT: That is not what I mean.

SOCRATES: So what do you mean?

KANT: We do not have to go into theology in order to justify ethics.

SOCRATES: So you *are* a pantheist, then?

KANT: As I said, we do not have to go into theology in order to justify ethics.

SOCRATES: So you are *not* a pantheist, then?

KANT: Were you listening, Socrates? We do not have to go into theology in order to justify ethics.

SOCRATES: But if the argument we have been following so far has led us reliably, it appears that we do.

KANT: I see no reason why we can't just stop at agreed rational morality, which is provable, and not enter the controversial and unprovable regions of theology.

SOCRATES: We could. But that would be an act of will, not of reason. We would then not be following the argument wherever it leads, like rafters following a river downstream, but we would be grounding our raft, halting the natural inquiry of the mind by an extrinsic act of the will—a heteronymous act of the will, so to speak. We could thus stop our discussion at our point of agreement that morality is absolute and intrinsic. But if we ask one more question, the question *why* this is so, we end up in disagreement about the role of God.

KANT: Well, where do *you* say, or where do your theistic friends say, that the absoluteness and authority of the moral law comes from?

SOCRATES: Not from the will of man, surely.

KANT: From the will of God, then?

SOCRATES: No. That is Euthyphro's position.

KANT: From the mind of man?

SOCRATES: No.

KANT: From the mind of God?

SOCRATES: No.

KANT: From what, then?

SOCRATES: They say it comes from God's own nature. As He Himself repeatedly explained to the people He chose and instructed in morality, according to their Scriptures: "You must be holy because the Lord your God is holy."

KANT: But those same Scriptures tell us that God created man in His own image and left him in the hands of his own counsel.

SOCRATES: There seems to be no necessary contradiction between those two teachings of your Scriptures. I am not qualified to interpret your Scriptures or to prove theological conclusions from them. But you seem to agree with traditional Christians about the absoluteness of conscience, whether or not it is God's prophet in the soul, as they say it is. But you do not seem to agree with them about the absoluteness of the authority of the God in Whose name that prophet speaks. For you, this God seems to be simply reason itself.

KANT: Let it be so, then. These are problems about God but not about man and conscience.

SOCRATES: No, I think there are problems there too.

KANT: What problem do you see about my concept of man's conscience?

SOCRATES: You say that morality is autonomous.

KANT: Yes.

SOCRATES: And you say that this means that man binds himself by the moral law.

KANT: Yes.

SOCRATES: That seems to be a self-contradiction. How can man's will be both the cause and the effect of moral obligation? How can the judge and the prisoner be the same person? It would seem that if we tie ourselves up, we can untie ourselves also, physically; and the same seems to hold morally: if we make a law, we can also unmake it.

KANT: I make a distinction. It is the empirical ego, the ego that we are aware of as a mental object, that is bound by the law. It is the transcendental ego, the ego that functions as a pure subject, the ego that is not an object of our awareness, that legislates the law.

SOCRATES: Your view of man seems schizophrenic, as if we had two egos rather than one.

KANT: No, it is one ego but it functions in two ways.

SOCRATES: But the two ways *seem* to contradict each other. Let's try to find out whether they really do or not. Let's see . . . you speak of the transcendental ego, and this is not meaningless speech, and to speak of anything meaningfully, we must think of it, isn't that so?

KANT: Yes, we must think of it in some way. Sometimes, we can know a thing only indirectly. And sometimes we can know a thing only negatively, as what it is not rather than as what it is. And sometimes we can know a thing only as a limit on the thinkable rather than as itself a thing thinkable.

SOCRATES: But in all of these cases, *however* you think of it, you do think of it. And to think of it is to know it in some way, to know something about it. Even if you know it only indirectly, or negatively, you know it well enough say it is distinguished from the empirical ego, don't you?

KANT: Yes.

SOCRATES: And that distinction, you say, is that the empirical ego can be known directly, as an object of consciousness, while the transcendental ego cannot —is that right?

KANT: Yes. It is the transcendental subject of consciousness.

SOCRATES: That sounds very much like the description of God, or Brahman, in the Hindu scriptures, the *Upanishads*: "the thinker of every thought", which, since it is thinker and not thought, can never be thought.

KANT: There is that parallel. But I do not identify it with Brahman, or with God, or with anything else. That would be to do transcendent metaphysics.

SOCRATES: I understand. But to think of something is, by definition, to have that something as the object of thought, is it not?

KANT: Yes.

SOCRATES: But you said it could not be an object of thought.

KANT: Once again I answer the charge of contradiction with a distinction. It is the distinction between the transcendent and the transcendental. The transcendent transcends our experience in the objective direction: it transcends all empirical objects. That is what I deny we can do. The transcendental transcends our experience in the subjective direction: it is the preconditions in the subject that make our experience possible, especially our rational and moral experience. And *that* I say we can know, and I say that I have shown how we can know it theoretically in *The Critique of Pure Reason* and practically and morally in

The Critique of Practical Reason and in the little book we are now discussing, the *Grounding.*

SOCRATES: I understand what you are doing in your transcendental method, and I do not deny that it is legitimate. But in speaking about the transcendental ego, you bring it out of its transcendental subjective hiding place, so to speak, and into the open light of objecthood, making it an object of your reflective thought.

KANT: I do this, indeed, but I do not see why you think it is a contradiction.

SOCRATES: That is a real change of status for it, so to speak, from the unknown subject to the known object.

KANT: Yes, of course it is. Where is the contradiction?

SOCRATES: Is it the same thing in both places?

KANT: Where are you going with this question, Socrates?

SOCRATES: If it is not the same thing in both places, both before and after you know it as an object, then you do not really know it, but something else.

KANT: That's true. So it *is* the same thing. It is the transcendental ego.

SOCRATES: Then, if so, you have succeeded in doing what you say in your *Critique of Pure Reason* cannot be done: knowing a thing-in-itself as it is in itself. For you know that it is transcendental, not transcendent. That is what it is in itself.

KANT: I think your argument is a purely verbal sophism, Socrates.

SOCRATES: No, it is not about words. It is about a real change. Just look at this change that happens to the transcendental ego when you know it, and think about it, and write about it. Consider the change from *before* it became known to *after*. Before you thought about it and wrote about it, the transcendental ego must have been acting, making possible your rational and moral experience, isn't that right?

KANT: Yes.

SOCRATES: But once you write about it, and think about it, you are now making it also an object of thought, which it was not before.

KANT: Of course.

SOCRATES: And that difference, the difference between the "before" and the "after", that change from being only a subject and not an object, into being also an object of philosophical reflection, via your "transcendental method", seems to be a self-contradiction. For you are saying that there is something—the "transcendental ego"—which not only is *not yet* an object but which differs from the empirical ego precisely by the fact that it *cannot* be an object. But to say that about it is to make it an object—an object of thought.

It is exactly like your "things-in-themselves" in your epistemology. I saw exactly the same self-contradiction there.

KANT: And I stand by my answer that I gave to you there: that it is no different from the knowledge of God, as explained by many traditional Christian, Jewish, and Muslim philosophers, such as Thomas Aquinas. They said that we can know *that* He exists without knowing *what* He is; that the existence of God is knowable by man, but not the divine essence. Now no one thought *that* was a self-contradiction. So if it is not a self-contradiction with regard to God, then neither is it a self-contradiction with regard to either things-in-themselves or the transcendental ego.

This is the point of my whole transcendental method, you see. We cannot get these things out in front of us, so to speak, and define what they are, but we can become aware that they are functioning behind us, like the sun casting shadows. We cannot look at the sun directly, but we can know it is there. The same is true for God as for the transcendental ego.

SOCRATES: Once again I have to ask you directly: Is the transcendental ego God, then? And if so, is it the God of theism or the God of pantheism?

KANT: That is a theological question.

SOCRATES: Of course it is. And it is a request for a theological answer.

KANT: I do not have one, Socrates. I do not know. I *believe* in the God of Christianity, and I do not claim to *know* the relation between this God and the God of Hinduism.

SOCRATES: Can you tell me anything about the relation between this God and the transcendental ego?

KANT: No.

SOCRATES: How sudden, dogmatic, and arbitrary your agnosticism seems to be!

KANT: I am constrained to it by my philosophy, Socrates. It is an honest agnosticism.

SOCRATES: I see. I suppose I will just have to accept your word on that.

Well, I also have another problem related to your notion of the autonomy of the will.

KANT: What is it?

SOCRATES: It is about the role of conscience. You do agree with the popular opinion that believes that our moral conscience informs us of good and evil, do you not?

KANT: You could say that that is one of the things conscience does, yes.

SOCRATES: Does it do this both in general and in particular?

KANT: What do you mean?

SOCRATES: I mean that the common opinion is that conscience tells us two things:

1. first, that *there is* a realm or dimension of good and evil in general;

2. and second, more particularly, it tells us *which things* are good and which are evil, which things to do and which not to do.

Most people before you thought that conscience did that particular task by some list of particular goods and evils like the Ten Commandments, but you say that it does that by the "categorical imperative". Isn't that so?

KANT: Yes. But conscience not only informs us about good and evil, but commands us to do good and not evil. That is its essential function. It legislates what ought to be rather than informing us about what already is. It is practical reason, not theoretical reason.

SOCRATES: And you say that it also legislates the moral law, or makes the moral law, or authors the moral law, do you not? Is that not the essential meaning of "autonomy"?

KANT: Yes. But I do not call this power "conscience". I call it the moral *will* of man.

"Conscience" contains the word "science". It sounds too intellectual.

SOCRATES: But it is man, it is the human rational soul, it is human "practical reason", that does this—isn't that correct?

KANT: Yes.

SOCRATES: Now is it the same power that both *informs* us of good and evil and *commands* the good? Or does that informing come from another power?

KANT: Not from another power. In constraining us, the practical reason also informs us.

SOCRATES: And does it inform us of the moral law both in general and in particular?

KANT: The general is sufficient. All particulars can be immediately deduced from the single "categorical imperative".

SOCRATES: That is also sufficient for my argument. So you say that the same power both informs us of morality and legislates morality, correct?

KANT: Yes.

SOCRATES: And by "legislating" you mean "*making the law*"?

KANT: Yes.

SOCRATES: Now when we are informed about anything, we receive form, do we not?

KANT: Yes. The empirical ego receives new form and determination. The point of my "Copernican revolution" is that all this form comes from the reason, not from the thing-in-itself.

SOCRATES: But you agree that the empirical ego receives form?

KANT: Yes—ultimately, it receives it from the transcendental ego, which makes the form.

SOCRATES: And we conform to that form which we receive, do we not? We are changed by it, are we not?

KANT: Yes.

SOCRATES: But when a legislator legislates, or makes a law, he *informs* rather than *conforms*, does he not? He creates rather than discovers.

KANT: Yes.

SOCRATES: How then can the same power both discover the moral law and also legislate it? It sounds like an author discovering a book that he himself wrote.

KANT: It is the distinction between the empirical ego and the transcendental ego again. That distinction holds true both in theoretical and practical reason.

SOCRATES: So these are two powers rather than one?

KANT: Yes.

SOCRATES: Well, then, I would like to know just how these two powers work together. Are there two distinct steps? Do you say that the informing, the legislating, the work of the transcendental ego, comes first? And then the being-informed, the standing-under-the-law, the work of the empirical ego, comes later?

KANT: Yes. But "later" not necessarily in time but in causality. The muscles in your legs cause your body to run, but there is no time gap between the act of the muscles and the act of running. A desk causes a book to remain off the floor at the same time as the book is caused to remain off the floor.

SOCRATES: I see. And this hidden work of the transcendental ego—is it the work of each individual?

KANT: The transcendental ego does its work in each individual, but it is the same for all individuals, so it is not simply the work of the empirical ego of each individual.

SOCRATES: Is it the work of all humanity collectively then?

KANT: No, for that is just as objectifiable as the empirical ego of an individual. And humanity collectively is just as subject to moral judgment as the work of any individual ego: all of humanity may sin or practice virtue just as much as one individual may. Both are informed and judged as objects.

SOCRATES: Is it the work of God, then?

KANT: No, for that would make it heteronymous.

SOCRATES: Is it then the work of something more than man but less than God, like the single "agent intellect" of the medieval Muslim philosophers?

KANT: No, for that is just as heteronymous as God.

SOCRATES: The only thing that seems to be left is something like the Hindu Atman— in which case you seem to be more of a pantheist than a theist.

KANT: I do not claim to solve the problems of theology, Socrates.

17

Free Will

SOCRATES: Let's proceed to your next step, which is to prove free will from your previous point, the will's autonomy. You say:

> **The concept of freedom is the key for an explanation of the autonomy of the will. . . .**   G 446
>
> **If freedom of the will is presupposed, morality (together with its principle** [autonomy]**) follows. . . .**   G 447
>
> [Therefore] **freedom must be presupposed as a property of the will of all rational beings.**   G 447

KANT: In other words, "Ought implies can."

SOCRATES: And "ought" means the fact that we are under a real and absolute moral obligation, a "categorical imperative"?

KANT: Exactly.

SOCRATES: And "can" means that we have the freedom to choose between obedience and disobedience to this moral imperative?

KANT: Exactly.

SOCRATES: And "ought implies can" because if we cannot choose this moral good, then we cannot be under obligation to choose it?

KANT: Exactly.

SOCRATES: So the argument is:

If I am not free to choose, I am not under moral obligation.
But I am under moral obligation.
Therefore I am free to choose.

KANT: That is indeed the argument. And it seems to me unanswerable, for both premises seem undeniable.

SOCRATES: Why is the first premise undeniable?

KANT: Because it is almost a tautology. It makes no sense to command stones or machines, however complicated they may be.

SOCRATES: Your argument there seems to be both strong and sound—though it is hardly original. But I think it is more complex than it seems. I think you have something else in mind than the two simple concepts of free will and moral obligation. I think you have in mind also what you have just called *autonomy* of the will. For you say not only that free will explains obligation but also that it explains autonomy.

KANT: I do.

SOCRATES: Now things are getting more complicated, since we have *two* kinds of freedom to deal with, free choice and autonomy. It's not just the simple, two-concept argument that "ought implies can", then, but we have this third factor of autonomy. Where do you factor that in?

KANT: What do you mean, "where"?

SOCRATES: Do you link autonomy of the will with the "ought" premise, that is, with moral obligation, or with its "can" conclusion, with free will?

You seem to link it with the "ought" premise, for you say **"morality (together with its principle) follows"**, and "its principle" here clearly means autonomy, does it not? That is the point you have just made.   G 447

KANT: Yes, that is what I mean.

But I think you misunderstand the logic of the argument, Socrates. When I say that "morality *follows*", I do not mean it follows by deductive logic, as "I am mortal" follows from "All men are mortal and I am a man." I mean that freedom of the will, freedom of choice, is a necessary cause, or rather a necessary *condition of possibility*, for morality, *and so also is autonomy*. They are both necessary conditions for morality.

SOCRATES: So autonomy is as much a necessary precondition of moral obligation as free will is?

KANT: Yes.

SOCRATES: Would you stand by this argument too, then?

> If we are not autonomous, we are not morally
>   obligated.
> But we are morally obligated.
> Therefore we are autonomous.

KANT: Yes.

SOCRATES: That argument seems much more questionable than the first one, which proved freedom of choice.

KANT: Naturally. For autonomy is a more hidden and more ultimate cause, or condition of possibility, for morality than is freedom of choice.

SOCRATES: It seems to be more than just hidden; it seems to be self-contradictory.

KANT: Why?

SOCRATES: Because the essential notion of obligation, and duty, seems to imply the *opposite* of autonomy, namely, being *under* moral law, while the notion of autonomy seems to imply the opposite of obligation: it seems to imply freedom from obligation.

KANT: Is this the argument you made a little while ago, Socrates, about informing versus being informed?

SOCRATES: Yes.

KANT: Then at the risk of being tediously repetitive, I must give you the same answer one more time. I distinguish the two functions of the ego: by the transcendental ego, we actively will the law and form it; and by the empirical ego, we are informed by it: we discover it and our obligation to it.

This is parallel to the two functions of the theoretical reason in my epistemology: the a posteriori mind that depends on the senses to be informed is a function of the empirical ego. But the a priori mind that informs the senses with time and space, and informs the logical mind with the twelve categories, and informs metaphysical consciousness with the Ideas of Pure Reason, is a function of the transcendental ego. Thus we (the empirical ego) discover the forms we (the transcendental ego) have already created.

SOCRATES: So your ethics does depend on your epistemology.

KANT: Indeed. You cannot tear apart the two parts of my philosophy.

SOCRATES: If that is so, then I must confess that I am disappointed, for I had hoped that I could do exactly that.

KANT: Why?

SOCRATES: Because from the viewpoint of common sense, your ethics makes a lot more sense than your epistemology. It is the disappointment of seeing a strong building on a weak foundation.

But I have one more question, and this one is about your *strategy*. You seem to try to prove free will not only from the premise of moral obligation but also from the premise of autonomy.

KANT: Yes, I do.

SOCRATES: That seems a strange strategy.

KANT: Why?

SOCRATES: Because it is trying to prove something that everyone, or nearly everyone, already believes from a premise that very few people believe, at least if they are not atheists or agnostics.

KANT: You misunderstand my strategy, Socrates. It is the strategy of a philosopher rather than a rhetorician. My aim is not to subjectively convince the most people, but to show the objective logic of the matter.

And even for the purposes of practical rhetorical strategy, I think I was right to argue in this way, since my argument will convince some people to believe in free will who otherwise would not. For there were a very significant number of people in my time, both philosophers and nonphilosophers, who denied the freedom of the will because science had discovered the causal mechanisms in nature that apparently necessitated everything. So to prove free will to these people was a strategically important achievement.

SOCRATES: Still, even granting that need to prove free will to the skeptics, would it not have been more effective to rest your whole case for free will on your first, simple argument above, that "ought implies can" rather than arguing from the more controversial premise of autonomy?

KANT: There is nothing wrong with adding a second argument to bolster your conclusion.

SOCRATES: True. But would it not have been even easier and more effective to have used as your second argument Aquinas' even simpler argument?

KANT: Which?

SOCRATES: That the meaningfulness of moral language implies free will. That if the will is not free to choose, then all moral language, all imperatives, and all human discourse that praises, blames, rewards, punishes, counsels, or commands is meaningless. It is

FREE WILL   301

meaningless to try to make a machine feel guilty and repent when it does not work well. We either repair it or throw it away.

KANT: Alas, I fear that some people will embrace that premise and deny both free will and the whole moral order; they will be all too willing to believe we have no free will and then act on that conclusion and its corollary about machines, trying to repair other people or throw them away rather than persuading them. For the temptation to treat others as objects of repair rather than as free subjects of choice is a very strong and subtle temptation. That is why we need my second formulation of the categorical imperative.

SOCRATES: I must second your "alas" with my own there, Immanuel. For in the centuries after you died, there will arise a significant number of dictators who exactly fit that description.

But I still question your strategy of using autonomy as a premise in the argument either for free will or for moral obligation. And I question this on practical grounds. For there will also appear after your time a number of "immoralist" philosophers who will embrace your notion of autonomy and use it to *erase* your notion of obligation—who will so identify the freedom of the will with the autonomy of the will that they will argue that

> If we are not autonomous, we are not free.
> And we are free.
> Therefore we are autonomous.
> But if we are autonomous, we are not obligated.
> Therefore we are not obligated.

KANT: The conclusion of that argument is not only false but backward. It is exactly the opposite: we are obligated only *because* we are autonomous.

SOCRATES: But most people will not agree with that, will they?

KANT: Probably not, not until they have read and understood my philosophy, at any rate.

SOCRATES: So common sense will say: If I am autonomous, I am *not* obligated.

KANT: Yes, but "common sense" is wrong there.

SOCRATES: But *whoever* is right and whoever is wrong about this, is it not a very dangerous thing to give these people a reason to be immoralists? Is it not like giving them a new weapon, like gunpowder, and telling them to use it rightly, but foreseeing that many of them will use it wrongly, but giving it to them anyway? That is exactly what Alfred Nobel did, and he so regretted it that he set up the Nobel Peace Prize to try to do reparation for the harm he did to humanity.

KANT: So you are saying that even if my idea is true it should not be taught?

SOCRATES: Not to everyone at all times, no.

KANT: That is a dangerous principle, Socrates: to suppress the truth because of human weakness and ignorance.

SOCRATES: I do not suggest that principle. I suggest merely that some truths can be taught too early, or too late.

KANT: Give me an example.

SOCRATES: The idea of predestination. It is in your Bible, so in some sense I think you believe that it is true. But even if it is true, it will probably be misunderstood and misused by many people who hear it too soon. Its proper use seems to be to give credit to God *after* a person has freely chosen to believe and to obey; but if it is taught too early, it will often be used as an excuse for *not* choosing to believe or obey, or for not choosing at all. For if all is infallibly predestined, even my choices, I can apparently simply lie back supinely and say, "What can I do? Whatever will be, will be."

KANT: I see your point in such cases. But I think my case is the opposite. I think the idea of the autonomy of will will purify moral motives.

SOCRATES: Perhaps so. But even if that is so, "purifying" is something that properly comes late, so to speak: something whose proper place is at the end of a process, is it not?

KANT: Yes. Like the idea of predestination.

SOCRATES: And therefore it would be improper if it came too early. So it would be right not to teach it to beginners.

KANT: That logically follows. But we are speaking here not of objective logic but of practical and prudential matters, about which we will never reach certainty, and about which we can only struggle forward hoping to find the best roads.

SOCRATES: That is true. And therefore I would like to get back to our properly logical arguments about free will. I want to investigate your reason for believing the three very practically important ideas of freedom of will, immortality, and God.

You said we could not prove any of these ideas by speculative reason, correct?

KANT: Yes.

SOCRATES: And you say now that they can all be proved by practical reason as necessary for morality, as the conditions of possibility for true morality.

KANT: That is correct.

SOCRATES: Could you explain that practical argument more specifically?

KANT: I will be happy to.

Unless we are free, we can neither legislate the moral law, as autonomy demands, nor choose to obey it, as moral duty demands.

Unless we are immortal, we cannot ever reach moral perfection, so hope is dashed, especially hope of justice, since perfect justice is rarely attained in this life.

And unless God exists, no real being realizes moral perfection, so that the ideal of perfect goodness is impossible and a mere abstract idea or wish.

God, freedom, and immortality are "postulates of practical reason". They are demanded by our moral needs. Thus I derive from the moral law these three great truths, which I could not derive from speculative reason.

SOCRATES: I understand your strategy. But I do not understand how God can be a "postulate" of the will. How can a postulate create the universe?

KANT: *God* is not a postulate; God is a real being. But our *belief* in God is a postulate rather than the conclusion of a valid demonstrative argument.

SOCRATES: You say we cannot prove God's existence.

KANT: Yes.

SOCRATES: And therefore we cannot know with certainty that He is real.

KANT: Not with our theoretical reason, no.

SOCRATES: But we can know that He is a necessary postulate for morality.

KANT: Yes.

SOCRATES: So without God, there could be no morality.

KANT: Ultimately, yes. No complete morality, no full morality, no adequate morality.

SOCRATES: In our first conversation about your ethics, I mentioned a famous remark of Dostoyevski to the effect that if God did not exist everything would be permissible. And you said you disagreed with that remark.

KANT: I do disagree with it.

SOCRATES: You also predicted, correctly, that it would be used by both atheists and theists. In fact, the atheists, especially a man named Sartre, and before him a man named Nietzsche, used it to argue this way:

If there is no God, everything is permissible.
And there is no God.
Therefore everything is permissible.

But the theists used the same premise in the opposite way, in a version of a very old argument for
the existence of God, the moral argument:

If there is no God, everything is permissible.
And not everything is permissible.
Therefore there is a God.

Now this "moral argument for the existence of
God" seems very similar to your argument for God
being morally necessary. And yet you do not agree
with its premise, Dostoyevski's saying. And you say
there *is* no proof for the existence of God, so this "if
. . . then" argument, even if you use it, cannot be a
proof of God's existence.

KANT: I do not consider it a proof. I say that God is
an a priori postulate for morality, not a demonstrated
conclusion.

SOCRATES: And even though both atheists and many
theists agree with Dostoyevski's saying, you do not.

KANT: No. But I'm not sure what Dostoyevski meant.
He seems to mean something like the "divine command theory" that Euthyphro held and that you
yourself refuted: the idea that God's will is the *cause*
of morality, of the moral law; that He is the legislator and the moral law is His effect. That "divine
command theory" is what I have rejected as "heteronomy".

SOCRATES: But not all forms of what you call "heteronomy" are the "divine command theory". Thinkers like Aquinas reject the "divine command theory" but they would also reject your theory of "autonomy".

Now even though you reject Dostoyevski's connection, you do affirm that there is a connection between God and morality.

KANT: Yes.

SOCRATES: And that it is a necessary connection.

KANT: Yes.

SOCRATES: So God is necessary for morality.

KANT: Yes, but not as its *cause* but as its *ideal*, its perfect end and goal and model. Not the efficient cause but the final cause.

SOCRATES: I wonder why you reduce the role of the Creator so radically. Surely if God did in fact create us in His image, it would follow that our will could not be the *first* cause of the moral law, but His will would be, if His will existed before our will and willed to create us—unless you maintain either that God did not create us or that God does not will morality.

KANT: I do not deny that God created us. And I do not deny that He wills us to be moral. But I deny that He wills the moral law into existence. That is the "divine command theory".

SOCRATES: So it is our will that wills the moral law into existence?

KANT: It is our will that legislates the moral law, yes.

SOCRATES: Then it seems you simply have a "human command theory" instead of a "divine command theory". And that would seem to be an even shakier foundation for morality.

But let me ask you about your reason for believing in God. You say we need God for a complete justification of morality, is that right?

KANT: Yes. It is a practical faith rather than a theoretical proof.

SOCRATES: But surely either God really exists or He does not.

KANT: Of course.

SOCRATES: And if He does not, we cannot will Him into existence, can we? Not for any reason at all, however necessary or moral it may be.

KANT: Of course not. I do not say we will Him into existence. *His existence* is not dependent on our will, but *our knowledge* of His existence is.

SOCRATES: I understand. But I still do not understand this; if He really does exist, and if He created us, how can our will be autonomous?

KANT: Because though He created us, He created us with free will. He put our fate into our own hands. He made us images of Himself, and since He is free, we are free.

SOCRATES: That is an answer, indeed. But it explains free will rather than autonomy. I think you confuse these two kinds of freedom. Nearly everyone can see that if we are truly under moral obligation, our will must be free from being completely determined by

efficient causes outside ourselves. But I do not see—
and neither do most people, I think—how our will
can be free of determination by *formal* causality, how
it can be a law unto itself, as you say.

KANT: It is *not* free of formal causality. Its formal
causality comes from the categorical imperative.

SOCRATES: But that, in turn, comes from the will. So
we seem to have a circle here. Our will determines
the very law that determines our will. How is that
circle broken?

KANT: The circle is broken by the fact that the will
first wills the form of the law, autonomously—and
only then does the law bind it. Similarly, the mind
first thinks the forms of the world that then informs
it. That is the parallel between my ethics and my
epistemology—again.

SOCRATES: Even though it is a perfect parallel, it still
seems circular. It is a parallel between two circles.

Let's see whether we can get to the bottom of this.

How do you answer this charge?—that when you
say that the will is the creator of the moral law, you
are confusing freedom of choice with freedom of independence? You seem to be assuming that we could
not really be free if we were under the law of another,
which you call "heteronomy".

Your strategy seems to be as follows:

To save moral duty and obligation you demand free
will. "Ought" implies "can".

And to perfect free will you demand autonomy.

But by demanding autonomy you seem to sacrifice
moral duty and obligation.

KANT: The first two statements are true, the third is not. I do not sacrifice moral duty and obligation by autonomy. I perfect it.

SOCRATES: But I still do not understand how we could be bound by a law we made ourselves. That sounds like tying yourself up in a chair, or locking yourself in a room but keeping the key. If you bind yourself, you can also release yourself. You have not yet explained that contradiction, I think.

KANT: But I think I have. It is not the individual will that legislates the moral law, but the universal will, will as such. It is the distinction between the transcendental ego and the empirical ego once again.

SOCRATES: And once again, I ask: Do we have two egos, two selves? Is the word "I" a lie?

KANT: No.

SOCRATES: Which ego am I, then? Which Socrates are you speaking to?

KANT: The empirical ego is what is now conscious and choosing and speaking.

SOCRATES: Then what is the transcendental ego? Is it God?

KANT: No.

SOCRATES: Is it Socrates?

KANT: No. It is not an individual.

SOCRATES: Is it a great, invisible, collective self, then? Is it Atman?

KANT: I do not say it is Atman.

SOCRATES: Then it seems to be a ghost. And you cannot found something as important as morality on a ghost.

KANT: How would *you* found morality?

SOCRATES: I don't know, but most people in your society would say that morality is founded more firmly and clearly by the traditional Christian or Jewish or Muslim religion than by your philosophy.

KANT: What do you mean by this traditional religion? Could you summarize it simply and clearly so that we can compare it with mine and see whether there are any significant differences?

SOCRATES: Fair enough. I will try to summarize it in four points.

First of all, it says that God is first of all—that God exists, and that God is the Creator, and that God created us, willed us into existence. And since for us to exist is ontologically good, and since God willed this, we can say that God's will is the source of our ontological goodness. And since willing the good of the other is the definition of love, or charity, or benevolence, we can say that God's will toward us is love, or benevolence, or charity, or goodwill. Let's call that Point number 1.

Point number 2 is that since benevolence wills not only the ontological good of the other but also the psychological good of the other, or happiness—true happiness, blessedness. So God wills our *happiness*. So happiness can be our end, as Aristotle says.

Point number 3 is that God wills our *moral* good, that He wills us to be virtuous. For the only way we can be happy is by being virtuous, as both Plato and Aristotle knew. So God wants us to become good so that we can become happy.

Point number 4 is that God wills us to *do* good as the only way to *become* good. Aristotle said that virtue comes only through practice, building up moral habits.

Now you give us a fine *formula* for doing good, your "categorical imperative". But you want us to *do* good (point number 4) without the virtuous habits, as Aristotle called them, the habits of *being* good (point number 3), and without the Aristotelian motive of happiness (point number 2), and without basing it on the religious foundation of God and God's creation and God's benevolence (point number 1). Surely these three foundations would ground your building more firmly?

KANT: I do not *deny* any one of those four things.

SOCRATES: But you do not bring them into your ethics. Your moral duty rests on abstract foundations: the categorical imperative alone. And then when you explore the source and foundation and cause of *that*, it turns out to be the human will rather than the divine will. So your foundation seems weaker than the traditional one, as man is weaker than God.

So your foundation seems weaker for these two reasons. First, you substitute the human will for the divine will, and, second, you give an abstract foundation for morality instead of a concrete one, a *law* instead of a *being*. You abstract from metaphysics and from anthropology, from God and from human nature, from virtues and vices and character and habits. If your goal was to found ethics on the *strongest* possible foundation, I wonder why you deliberately *weakened* the traditional one in these ways.

KANT: The traditional religious foundation for morality may be *ontologically* stronger, but I say it is not *logically* or *epistemologically* stronger. It cannot be proved by speculative, theoretical reason. It cannot be known with certainty. I wanted to construct an absolute and certain ethics; that's why I confined myself to the parameters of reason alone—and of *practical* reason alone, for I believe that practical reason can do much more than theoretical reason. I cut down the bushes and weeds of theoretical reason to make room for the garden of practical faith.

SOCRATES: So both your structure and your strategy depend on your epistemology of theoretical reason. Your ethics depends on your epistemology.

KANT: Yes. We have already established that.

SOCRATES: Then I fear it is a beautiful building with a questionable foundation.

KANT: That is your final judgment on my work?

SOCRATES: Alas, it is.

KANT: I have two questions I would like to ask you in conclusion, if they are allowed.

SOCRATES: We do not forbid questions here.

KANT: You have told me what *you* think of my philosophy. Can you assure me that God agrees with your judgment on my philosophy?

And can you tell me His judgment on me? On how I am known to God? Can you tell me my Heavenly identity?

SOCRATES: Can I do these two things? I can answer both of those questions with the same answer.

KANT: And the answer is . . . ?

SOCRATES: I. Kant.

18

Kant's Philosophy of Religion and Politics

KANT: Are we finished, or must I endure more of your terrible puns in my Purgatory?

SOCRATES: Neither. But I would like to ask you a little more about your philosophy of religion.

KANT: Then my Purgatory is not over. Why?

SOCRATES: Because most religious people will find your notion of autonomy not only logically problematic but religiously scandalous, even blasphemous.

In your epistemology, you seem to have man take the place of God by being the author of all form, meaning, order, and design in the universe. And in your ethics, you seem to have man take the place of God by being the author of the moral law. Most religious people would probably find the first two-thirds of your ethics acceptable, even wonderful—I mean your first two imperatives—but when you reach the end, the summit, of your ethics, the imperative of autonomy, I think those who cheered your first two imperatives would blanch with horror at your third one.

KANT: That may be true, but it does not prove I am wrong.

SOCRATES: No, it does not. But it does mean you must provide a defense against an anticipated attack.

KANT: I do so by diagnosing the origin of that attack. It comes from a traditional religious assumption, which I question. The assumption is that subservience is essential to religion. I maintain that this assumption is not essential but accidental to religion as such. It comes from confusing religion with heteronomy, which is not the essence of religion as such but only its childhood, and which is *contrary* to the essence of religion once that child is grown to maturity.

SOCRATES: And have you grown to maturity?

KANT: I like to think so.

SOCRATES: Now there, I think, your problem lies. I say this only as an agnostic, but as one who is convinced that all people can be classified as either fools who think they are wise or the wise who think they are fools, as sinners who think they are saints or saints who think they are sinners, as children who think they are adults or adults who think they are children.

KANT: I disagree with your classification, Socrates. Adults can and should know that they are adults, and not think that they are children.

SOCRATES: But did not the Teacher you call your own say that unless you become as little children you cannot enter His Kingdom?

KANT: We are not arguing philosophically now, Socrates.

SOCRATES: Then let us do that. Let us define our terms, beginning with the term "religion". Most people would claim that that very "heteronomy and subservience" that you want to grow out of is precisely the very core and essence of religion. Muslims call it "islam": surrender, submission to the will of God, the Infinite Other. I think most religious Jews and Christians would agree with the Muslims there, about the definition of the universal essence of religion.

You, on the other hand, say in your *Grounding* that this "heteronomy" is the origin of all inauthentic morality, and I suspect you also say it is the origin of inauthentic religion too. Is this not so?

KANT: Yes, that is so.

SOCRATES: And your reason is that traditional religion reflects the heteronomy of the child while modern "enlightened" religion reflects the autonomy of an adult?

KANT: I believe that, yes. And I think I can explain my philosophy of religion to you by my philosophy of politics, and my philosophy of history.

SOCRATES: An unusual approach. Go ahead, please.

KANT: I believe that modernity represents an immense progress over ancient and medieval times, in philosophy as well as in science and technology. And one of the primary steps in that progress is in political philosophy, in the repudiation of the notion that the primary purpose of government is the *happiness* of its citizens. I say that the primary purpose of government is the assertion and defense and protection of their *rights*.

SOCRATES: This is a nice parallel to your point in ethics: you think that Aristotle's traditional ethics is wrong for labeling happiness the greatest good, and you replace it with an ethic centering on rights and duties instead.

KANT: Yes. Let me read what I have written. (A copy of my book entitled *On the Common Saying: This May Be Right in Theory, but It Is No Good in Practice* has just appeared in my hand, opened to the page I seek):

OCS

If a government is built on the principle of benevolence similar to that of a *father* towards his children, that is, a *paternal government* . . . , in which subjects are treated like children who have not yet come of age and who cannot distinguish what is truly beneficial from what is harmful for them . . . this is the greatest *despotism* imaginable. . . . Not a *paternal* but a *patriotic* government . . . is the only government conceivable for human beings who are capable of rights.

You see, Socrates, if the end of the state is the happiness of its citizens, its citizens are like the children of a father; and this means they are not free, even if it is a benevolent father.

SOCRATES: So freedom is incompatible with dependence?

KANT: Of course. And so is human dignity.

SOCRATES: Dignity resides in autonomy and indignity in heteronomy?

KANT: Yes. Surely you know the origin of the two words. In your ancient Greece, a city free to live under the laws it made itself was called "autonomous", which means literally "under the law (nomos) of itself (auto)", while a state that was captured by and enslaved to another state was called "heteronymous" because it was compelled to live by the law (nomos) of the other (hetero).

SOCRATES: So even if the paternal state is benevolent and charitable and does not use its citizens as mere means, even if such a state obeys your second imperative, it is still slavery unless there is autonomy, unless it progresses to your third imperative.

KANT: That is precisely my contention, yes. In fact, such a submission to a benevolent state is an even worse tyranny than submission to a cruel and oppressive state.

SOCRATES: What an astonishing thing to say! A benevolent tyrant is worse than a cruel one?

KANT: Yes. For submission to a benevolent tyrant is an interior submission, a submission of heart. A slave, by contrast, can still own his own heart and keep it free, even while his body is forced into servitude. But a son's heart is not his own; it belongs to his father.

SOCRATES: Do you see a child's submission to his father as inherently servile?

KANT: Not while the child is a child. But when he is an adult, yes.

SOCRATES: So your politics, and also your religion, depends on the assumption that mankind has come of age some time between the end of the Middle Ages and the eighteenth century, your century.

KANT: Yes.

SOCRATES: I see now why you suggested we look at your political philosophy as a means of understanding your philosophy of religion.

This "progressive" judgment of yours—is it a priori or a posteriori?

KANT: A posteriori, of course.

SOCRATES: And is it disputed?

KANT: Indeed it is, by conservatives both religiously and politically.

SOCRATES: In your Preface to the *Grounding for the Metaphysics of Morals*, you rejected any a posteriori basis for your ethics, such as any anthropology, any theory of human nature and a "natural law" based on it, such as Aristotle's, because it was a posteriori and therefore disputable. You demanded a "pure" philosophy of a priori truths with no disputable assumptions. But surely all historical, political, and ideological assumptions are highly disputable. I do not see how you can base your philosophy of religion on such disputable ideological assumptions as the judgment that mankind has finally come of age in the eighteenth century and thrown off the bondage of millennia of religious servitude.

KANT: I do not base my philosophy of religion on that religious assumption.

SOCRATES: But when pressed, you do.

KANT: And I do not see that assumption as "highly disputable".

SOCRATES: But it is highly, and passionately, disputed, especially by religious people. What you said about the "slavery" or "servitude" of submission to a benevolent father quite naturally sounded shocking, even blasphemous, to Christians who remembered the one and only prayer Christ gave His disciples: the prayer that tells them to call God their "Father". If we were to apply your principles to that, we would have to judge Christ to have been the most influential of all slave masters whose teachings held back human dignity and autonomy forever.

KANT: No, no. Why do you say "forever"?

SOCRATES: If God is eternal and unchanging, His fatherhood over mankind must be forever. For however much mankind may grow, it will never grow into equality with God, as a son grows into equality with his human father. Or do you say we can some day reach this goal? That some day we will create a universe?

KANT: I do not say that. But I do not interpret the fatherhood of God in that way. You have satirized my philosophy of religion rather than allowed me to explain it.

SOCRATES: If so, I apologize. And I beg you to explain it.

KANT: Thank you. I will try to be brief.

SOCRATES: For that, it is my turn to thank you.

KANT: Here is my essential argument the two fundamental points of religion, God and immortality.

The complete and total good for a human life is the combination of the lesser kind of good and the greater kind of good, the combination of happiness and moral virtue. Happiness consists in all the goods that come *to* us, while moral virtue consists in the good that comes *from* us, from our will, from a will that always seeks to do its duty. Happiness is the goal of the irrational inclinations, the satisfaction of all desires together. Moral virtue is the good of the practical reason. Virtue is under our control, happiness is not. Virtue comes from our free choice; happiness comes from divine providence or chance.

SOCRATES: So far what you say sounds very reasonable.

KANT: Now this is how I argue for a rational faith in immortality: Unless there is a life after death, no one can ever reach perfect virtue, for no one reaches it in this life.

SOCRATES: That is an interesting argument.

KANT: And here is another. Perfect justice is not done in this life, because we are not properly rewarded for our virtue with happiness.

SOCRATES: Plato tried to argue that we *were*, in the *Republic*.

KANT: And I think he failed. So there is the moral need for the next life for the sake of justice.

SOCRATES: Another interesting argument—but hardly an original one. How does God come in?

KANT: This is how I argue for a rational faith in God. There is the need for a God for almost exactly the same reason as there is a need for immortality: unless there is a God who combines *power* over the events of our lives with perfect *wisdom* and perfect *goodness*, both justice and benevolence, we will not be justly rewarded with happiness for our pursuit of virtue. For in this life many things happen to us by chance, not by justice.

SOCRATES: So the role of God is to see to it that there is immortality, in which justice will be done and we will be compensated for the injustices of this life?

KANT: That is not the only role of God.

SOCRATES: But it is the most important one?

KANT: Yes, since justice and moral goodness are more important than anything else.

SOCRATES: What are the other roles you allow to God?

KANT: What do you mean?

SOCRATES: Does your God also issue commandments?

KANT: No.

SOCRATES: Does He enter into a covenant relationship with His people?

KANT: What do you mean? How do you interpret that?

SOCRATES: Is he their benevolent Father?

KANT: Only when we are children.

SOCRATES: Is He in Himself their final cause and end and goal and happiness?

KANT: I said that He justly gives them happiness as the reward for their virtue.

SOCRATES: But is He also the intrinsic and formal cause of their happiness, as distinct from the extrinsic efficient cause of their happiness? Does their happiness consist essentially in union with Him?

KANT: No. That would be heteronomy again.

SOCRATES: Does He offer His grace as a means and union with Himself in Heaven as the end?

KANT: No, not when they are adults. Again, that is heteronomy.

SOCRATES: Then I fear that Jews and Christians who believe their Scriptures will have to conclude that your God is not the same God as theirs.

KANT: But in another sense I say Yes to all those questions of yours. For God freely offers His Kingdom to His people, to "whosoever will". But His Kingdom is a moral kingdom, a kingdom of persons as ends. It is the kingdom I wrote about in my *Grounding*, the community of persons that constitute what I called "the kingdom of ends". In this kingdom, each person is the end and not just a means. In a sense, each person is the King.

SOCRATES: Can you tell me more clearly what you mean by that? Surely you do not mean that each man is God?

KANT: No, we are not all God, but we *are* all gods.

SOCRATES: I am still not sure what that means.

KANT: Read what I have written. Here is my description of that kingdom, from *Religion within the Bounds of Reason Alone*:

> **That which alone can make a world the object of divine decree and the end of creation is *Humanity* . . . *in its full moral perfection*, from which happiness follows in the will of the Highest Being. . . . This man, who is alone pleasing to God** ["This is my beloved Son in whom I am well pleased" (Mt 3:17)], **"is in Him from all eternity"** ["The Word was with God" (Jn 1:1)]; **the idea of man proceeds from God's being; man is not, therefore, a created thing but God's only-begotten Son (Jn 1:18; 3:16-18), "the Word (the Fiat!) through which all other things are, and without whom nothing that is made would exist" (Jn 1:1-3) . . . for him . . . everything was made** ["All things were created through him and for him" (Col 1:16)].

RB

SOCRATES: Surely Christians will find this not just problematic and confusing but blasphemous. Especially the statement that **"man is not a created thing"**. And **"man is . . . God's only-begotten Son"**. What they identify as Christ, you identify as us. So we are really the second Person of the Trinity.

KANT: I do not use Trinitarian formulas.

SOCRATES: I see that. And I think I also see why.

KANT: Why?

SOCRATES: Because according to Christianity, even the Trinity is not autonomous. Each of the Persons eternally surrenders Himself to the others.

KANT: "Surrender" is primitive, childish language.

SOCRATES: Then love, in your philosophy, is primitive and childish too. For that is the language of love. And, I think, that is why your philosophy would make a Christian not just suspicious but appalled.

KANT: Traditional, medieval-style Christians, perhaps. Modern Christians, no.

SOCRATES: What is the essential difference between the two, in your mind?

KANT: As I said, modern Christians are adult Christians, those who have come of age.

SOCRATES: And therefore no longer are dependent on the Father?

KANT: They look up to the Father as their ideal, but they do not look back to Him in dependence.

SOCRATES: In other words, autonomy.

KANT: Yes. That is my last word on the subject.

SOCRATES: That is precisely why traditional religious people, religious Jews and Muslims as well as Christians, would be appalled. According to all three of those religious traditions, that was Satan's last word on the subject too, when he rebelled: "I will not serve." You see, in these religions, it is God Who is supposed to have the last word.